# MODELLING
# AND
# SCULPTURE

*A Guide for Artists and Students*

by

## EDOUARD LANTERI

*With a New Introduction*
*by Nathan Cabot Hale, sculptor*

*IN THREE VOLUMES     VOLUME II*

DOVER PUBLICATIONS, INC., NEW YORK

Published in Canada by General Publishing Company, Ltd., 30 Lesmill Road, Don Mills, Toronto, Ontario.
Published in the United Kingdom by Constable and Company, Ltd., 10 Orange Street, London W. C. 2.

This Dover edition, first published in 1965, is an unabridged and unaltered republication of the work first published by Chapman & Hall, Ltd. under the former title, *Modelling*. Volume I was first published in 1902, Volume II in 1904, and Volume III in 1911.
A new Introduction has been written specially for this Dover edition by Nathan Cabot Hale.

*Standard Book Number: 486-21419-2*
*Library of Congress Catalog Card Number: 65-25704*

Manufactured in the United States of America

Dover Publications, Inc.
180 Varick Street
New York, N. Y. 10014

# PREFACE

By all students of Sculpture, Professor Lanteri's admirable book must be welcomed with enthusiasm. At a time when it is more or less the fashion in many Art Schools to admit "impressionism," alas! even in the noble and restrained Art of Sculpture, it is indeed refreshing to read these pages, written not only with healthy vivacity, but with a thoroughness of knowledge, aye, more, a scientific insight uncommon in a tentative and experimental period of both teaching and learning.

It is the more satisfactory as coming from the Professor of the Royal College of Art, whose school therein has produced so many admirable sculptors, and where at this moment all the sound principles so elaborately set forth in this book are being practically initiated. When I say practically initiated I mean that there is no axiom illustrated on these pages which is not forcibly maintained in practice in the school which is lucky enough to have Professor Lanteri as Professor. I would rather call my preface a "tribute" than an introduction: a tribute in the sense of keen admiration for the industry, the success, and the stimulating cause which are such worthy elements in the Professor's teaching.    Enthusiasm is a great deal in a teacher : without that quality he is a lifeless block, may be, of erudition, but when erudition, may I say in these days of hurry, and classical thoroughness is combined with the power of inculcating enthusiasm, then a rare and very perfect teacher is found.    Words may be very picturesque, oratory may be perfect, rhetoric catching, but without the balance of sound reasoning and practical common sense, they are as the leaves of the Sibyl which were blown away from out her cave, leaves perhaps full of wisdom, but disconnected with each other and therefore useless.    Sculpture is so noble an Art that it cannot be played with ; it is an Art which demands scientific investigation, which demands real knowledge, not ephemeral or subsidiary, but lasting and essential.    We cannot guess at form nor can we fluke excellence when dealing with masses and planes of infinite intersections and varieties : the initiating steps must be sound and safely erected.    In this nature Sculpture has a close affinity with Architecture, it is structural, if it is not it is worthless.    To the amateur it is easy to produce some effect, just as it is easy to make a good deal of a few well-chosen sentences in a foreign language, but the fraud is very easily and very soon discovered, and the amateur sculptor and linguist remain so to the end of time.

# Preface

This book is one that ought to warn superficial students that they must labour, that the Art of Sculpture is so difficult and exacting in demands of accuracy as well as of good taste, that before entering in her fields, it may be well to remember that ancient saying in a very wise Book not sufficiently studied, " Take off thy shoes from off thy feet, the ground on which thou standest is holy ground."

It is as if Professor Lanteri had that motto before his mind when he prepared these pages of words and illustrations. He has approached his subject seriously, religiously, as a teacher and as a workman ; his readers must read, mark, learn, in the same spirit of reverence for the Art of which Lanteri is so distinguished an ornament.

Though I am a painter by trade, as colloquialism would express it, the other great sister Arts, Architecture and Sculpture, have, from my boyhood, in a measure, run alongside of my craftsmanship as a painter ; had this not been so, I should not have ventured to use my pen on this occasion.

I know the difficulties, I know the charms, I know the mazes into which the mysterious spirit of Form may lead or mislead.

I know that it is useless to model, except in the highest degree unsatisfactorily, without a sound and complete know-ledge of the human form.   Not only anatomically, but may I say decoratively, must the figure be studied part by part, and as a whole also. The many and ever deviating sections, the innumerable interlacing of planes, the endless varieties of surfaces, which go to make infinite and complicated outlines, must be studied not only by the eye generally, but by the mind specifically : and this is no easy task. " Impressionist mists" and "Will-o'-the-wisp" suggestions will lead and mislead till humility is taught to the student by finding himself floundering in a slough of despond : he may perhaps call for the Pedant, who has been his *bête noir*, to save him, and in modesty perhaps say, " If I had followed your track when I was foolish and vain, I might have found the 'delectable mountains'"; the Pedant, kind and indulgent, will take the foolish wanderer by the hand and set him into a straight road. The word Pedantry may be used in the sense of abuse, it may also imply the cause of final success. Students should be pedantic, narrow if you like, prejudiced if you will, positive also, but in the lines which their predecessors have laid down for them by centuries of labour and experience, and not guided by their own vagaries, which at the bottom of them have nothing but emotion. Let us feel, yes, feel intensely, but we can only be artists when reason and emotion have joined hands, the one guiding, the other impelling. And this principle I take it to underlie all that the author seeks to enforce. All character, all reason, every form and combination of forms contain combinations of emotions which Art can convey, but the artist is

powerless to convey them until he has trained himself to understand how and why certain combinations are impressive, either
by rhythm or sudden transitions. It is I think not the least
admirable chapter which deals with Composition. Composition
can be taught, originality cannot; the original student is sometimes held back by his originality, it may impede his progress,
because the initiating vision is so strong that he is apt to rush
into its embrace regardless of the pitfalls between him and it.
For the original genius, pedantry is probably as essential as to
the student less endowed ; it serves as a *check* upon his over
ardent and sanguine nature ; it acts as a balance against heed-
less or even reckless novelty.

Professor Lanteri in the long course of years has instructed
so many students that he probably knows better than most of
us do that " the genius " is not of necessity the individual who
in the long run does best ; though of a certainty he will do
best if he submits to authority in his student days. It is
especially for the cleverest fellows that this book must prove
of so much service. The experience in these pages is enormous, every possible pitfall has its fence round it, and every
imprudent step which a student might take will find therein a
guide which will land him at least somewhere ; and somewhere is a long way upon the road to excellence, because it
means that a goal has been attained with a purpose, and by an
effort which has been sustained and thorough. What more

can I say except to wish my friend Lanteri the success he deserves, and that success will appeal to him most warmly which will be gained by his students under his generous and able tuition.    If one might suggest a motto, might it not be a repetition of Michael Angelo's : "Sempre Imparo!"

W.  B.  RICHMOND.

# CONTENTS

## CHAPTER I

# Contents

## CHAPTER II

# Contents

# Contents

## MEDALS

# Contents

## COMPOSITION

# Contents

# Contents xvii

# Contents

# MODELLING

## CHAPTER I

### RELIEF FROM NATURE

When we model a study in the round, we must, as soon as the pose and action are arranged, obtain the proportion and construction of the figure. In modelling a relief, which is an interpretation of nature, we can, on the contrary, only gradually by our work obtain the appearance of this construction.

The effect of perspective has to be produced by a superposition of planes. These alone can give to a flat surface the appearance of roundness which the object possesses in nature.

The study of relief offers therefore much greater difficulties than the work in the round, which is a positive thing, whilst in relief,—beyond the outline of the figure, which remains the same as in the model, all the rest is artifice.

It is a grave mistake to let young beginners work in low-relief, as I have often seen it done! In order to do relief-studies, one must already be well acquainted with the construction of the human frame (only to be taught by studies in the round) so that we may suggest the construction by the more or less artificial means employed for relief.

Measures taken with the callipers are of as little use in relief as in drawing; for there is the perspective to be considered, which loses the true proportion pertaining to all the parts of the body.

The lower the relief, the greater the difficulty! Unless, the student is content to draw an outline on the background, and to fill it in with a certain quantity of clay, laid on in an even thickness, and then to put into this mass a few anatomical details. At that rate any one can do it,—but that is not true study from nature.

There is no absolute law for relief, it may be more or less projecting, and the sculptor must choose the degree of projection, which, for decorative purposes, depends on the place to be occupied by the work. Its projection, treatment and style ought to be governed by the architectural surroundings and by the height at which it will be placed.

In no case must the relief by too rich effect, or too much movement of lines, destroy the architecture that surrounds it, for from the decorative point of view its object is only to enhance the architectural effect.

I have seen plenty of such examples, where the sculptor seems to struggle with the architect to draw attention to his work only ;—a vulgar mistake, for the result is always destructive of the harmony of the whole.

I also know several cases, where, in order to enrich the effect of the relief, the sculptor has not hesitated to cut into the wall, even almost through the wall, to produce a violent shadow, darker than the strongest shadow of the whole architectural work which he is decorating ; so that unity and harmony are so completely destroyed as to alarm the mind of the spectator about the solidity of the structure ; for where the eye does not receive the impression of strength and possible duration, there is an unconscious misgiving, which will prevent the work of art from entirely satisfying us, however much we may admire it.

The Greek sculptors of the best epoch have never committed such mistakes, on the contrary, they more than any others have applied themselves to respect the principle, that the whole is more than the part.

Therefore in any relief designed for decorative purposes, we must above all harmonise the effect, that is the lights and shadows, as well as the style and lines of the composition with those of the surrounding architecture.

In beginning our first study of relief from nature we have to trouble about nothing except the projection which we judge to be appropriate to the pose and the character of the model. To begin with I should advise the relief to be rather high, that is about an inch of projection for the highest parts. That will allow you to accentuate the principles which I shall try to explain further on.

The object of our study in relief is to suggest in its slight projection as much as possible the effect of nature, not only in the outer contours, but also in producing the idea of roundness.

In decoration you cannot treat every pose in relief; limbs in perspective are not suitable for it, for, although they may be successfully executed, at a distance the result will be hardly intelligible, but rather confused and painful to look at.

Observe with what care Phidias has avoided all poses in perspective in his frieze of the Parthenon.

All the same it will be a good exercise, after some first studies of simple action, to make others with slight foreshortenings, as in a composition there may happen to be some foreshortenings that cannot be avoided without destroying the lines of the composition.

For a first study I advise the student to give his model a very simple pose, where the limbs will be presented as much as possible in their entire length, but yet with some

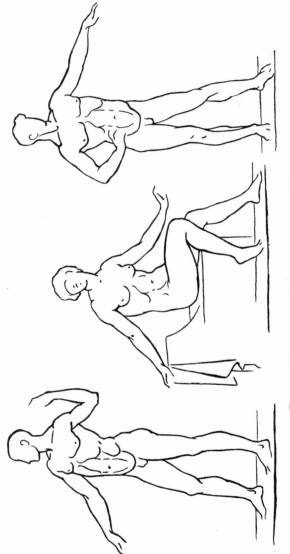

Fig. 1.—Example of Poses suitable for Relief.

contrasts in the large planes, as for instance in the direction of the plane of the upper or thoracic part of the figure with that of the lower or abdominal part of the torso, as well as the plane of the head in contrast with that of the thorax. (See example of poses in Fig. 1.)   However simple the pose,

the difficulty will be sufficiently great to make the study interesting.

Having posed the model, you make a clay background about 32 inches high and of a width according to the development of the pose.   This proportion is best for a first study ; you will gradually go on to the natural size.

Fix this background to the modelling-stand by means of two battens, their upper end nailed to the top of the board, the lower one to the turntable, see Fig. 2.

Fig. 2.

It is very essential to place the background vertically on the stand in order to get your figure well balanced, Fig. 3. If the bottom of your background projected beyond the upper part, you would put too much clay on the upper part of the figure in order that it should meet the plumb-line, and should the relief afterwards be placed in a vertical position,

the figure would fall forward. If the upper part of your
background should overhang, the opposite result would
happen. See Figs. 4, 5, 6, and 7.

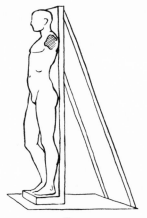

FIG. 3.

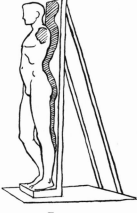

FIG. 4.

FIG. 5.

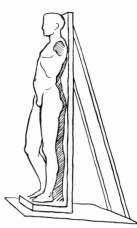

FIG. 6.

FIG. 7.

This settled, you draw with a modelling-tool on the clay background the pose of the figure in its larger lines, that

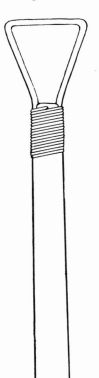

is, as for the figure in the round, the chief line of movement, the line of contrast of the shoulder with the iliacs, and so on. (Fig. 8.) I shall not here repeat the principles of the movement which I have already described in the first volume.

Now you fill this clay outline in to the maximum of relief that you wish to give to the figure (Fig. 9). The drawing has fixed the contrast of lines and the general direction of the movement, and now you attend to the contrasts of planes.

With a large wire-tool like Fig. 10 you firmly cut the large surfaces in their general direction and without reckoning with details (see Fig. 11); after these large planes you go on to the lesser ones according to their importance and thus come gradually to the details.

FIG. 10.

There is another way of making a relief of one inch projection: You make a background of two inches thickness, on which you draw the chief line and the

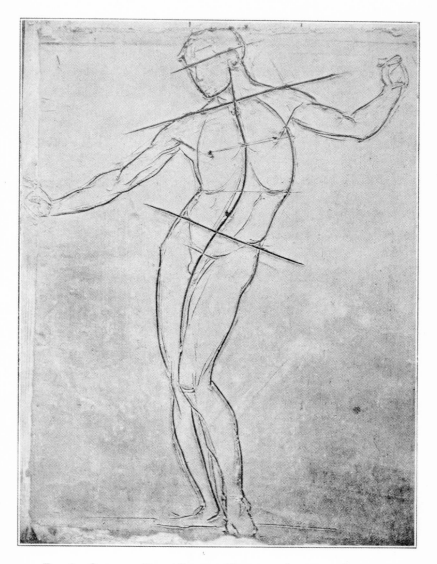

FIG. 8.—SHOWING CHIEF LINE OF POSE AND LINES OF CONTRAST.

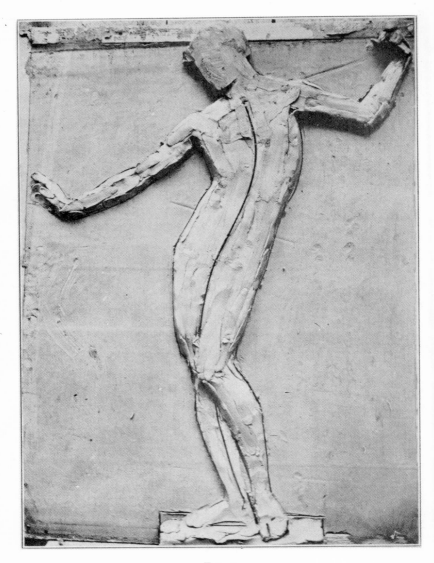

FIG. 9.

FIG. 11.—SHOWING THE LARGE SURFACES.

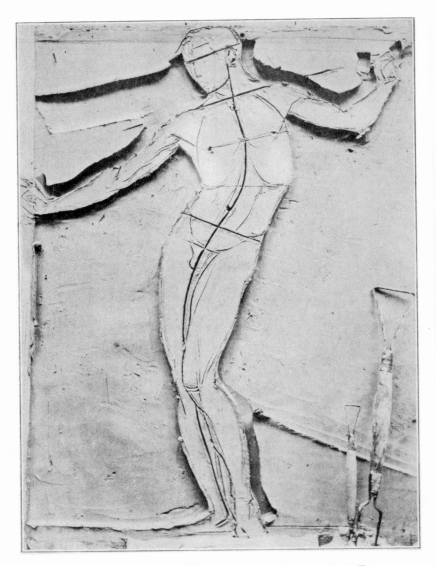

FIG. 12.—COMPARE THIS METHOD WITH THAT SHOWN IN FIG. 9.

outlines with a wire tool to the depth of one inch (Fig. 12), and then cut off the planes as before-mentioned. You will obtain the same result as by the first process and perhaps attain it more rapidly.

Both these ways of working are equally good for a relief of one inch depth, but the latter is preferable for a very low relief and not permissible for a higher relief than one inch.

The essential thing to be obtained one way or the other is the general substance of the figure. If you begin by indicating the head, then the neck, the thorax, and so on to the feet, by trying to give immediately the relation of planes and forms to each other, there will always be a lack of unity in the relation of the planes worked in that piecemeal fashion ; they seem not to blend and you will sometimes dig into the background or get so much projection that it will approach the actual form in the round ; in short, the sense of continuation and construction is lost from the beginning.

Having to give a flat surface the idea of natural roundness, we can only by lucky, that is, not readily perceptible deceptions get a successful effect, but our principal aim must be to obtain this by the superposition of planes, particularly in the outlines of the figure.

As I said before, if you are content with drawing an

outline, filling it in with clay to a certain thickness and indicating in this mass some divisions of form, you will produce the effect of a paper doll cut in outline and stuck on a background. It will be inert and cannot for a moment suggest either the construction or the atmosphere which surrounds the living model, because it has apparently only one plane, or rather two : that of the figure and that of the background.

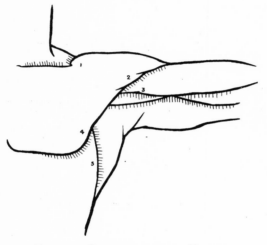

FIG. 13 —SUPERPOSITION OF PLANES.

To avoid this result, the most important principle in relief is to attend to the superposition of planes in the outer contours, and then to the inner outlines given by the various forms of the figure.

In Fig. 13, which represents the Deltoid, Trapezius, Biceps, Thorax and Dorsal, you will observe that the contours around these muscles present five superpositions of planes :

1. The Deltoid is outlined in projection over the Trapezius muscle.

2. The Deltoid is projecting over the Biceps.

3. The Biceps is outlined over the Coraco-Brachialis and over the Triceps.

4. The Pectoral is outlined above the Thorax.

5. The Thorax lies over the Dorsal.

---

Suppose we let the student gain this experience for himself, that is, make only one big contour round this mass of muscles without any superposition of muscles within the outline, and let him blend all the planes together as shown in Fig. 14 ; then on a fresh background exaggerate the prin-

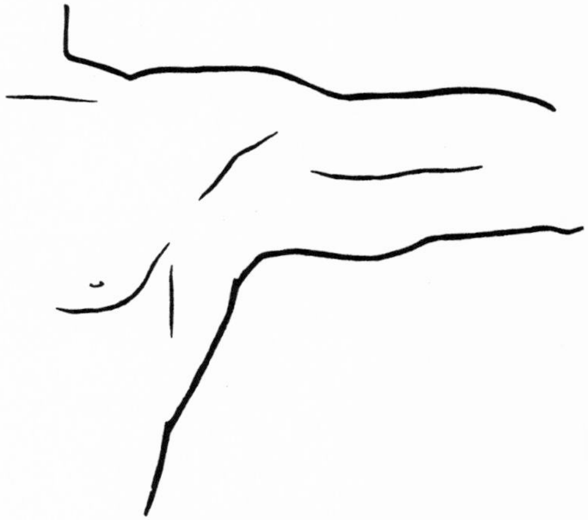

Fig. 14
Compare with Fig. 13.

ciple of superposition. He will immediately perceive the difference of strength in the form and the effect of distance which every higher plane gives to the adjoining one. He will notice the suggestion of roundness to be obtained, when each plane serves as foil to the other,—whilst with the previous attempt the effect from the distance is only that of the paper-doll stuck on a background.

This principle repeats itself in all the contours formed by the human figure. If you take the leg, (Fig. 15), in the interior outlines you will find, although perhaps less accentu-

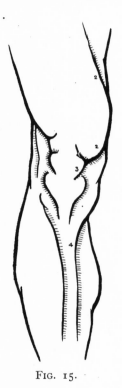

FIG. 15.

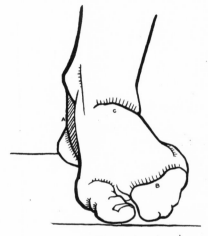

FIG. 16.

ated than in other parts, the following superpositions :

1. The Sartorius is outlined over the internal mass of the various Adductor muscles of the thigh.

2. The Vastus Internus (part of the great Triceps of the leg) is outlined against the Sartorius and the mass formed by the inner Condyle of the Femur and the head of the Tibia.

3. The Patella stands out over this same mass.

4. The Tibia is outlined against the Gastrocnemius.

In the foot seen from the front, as in Fig. 16, you will easily notice the following superpositions :—

(*a*) The interior profile of the Instep over the heel,

(*b*) The plane formed by the mass of the toes over the Metatarsus,

(*c*) The outline of the arch against the leg and the external ankle-bone.

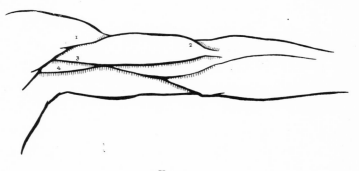

FIG. 17.

Let us also look at the inner view of the arm. There we find :

1 The Deltoid overlying the Biceps,

2. The Biceps over the mass of the Supinators,

3. The Biceps over the Coraco-Brachialis and Triceps,

4. The Coraco-Brachialis over the Triceps. (See Fig. 17.)

You will see from these examples, that this principle extends to all the exterior and interior contours of planes which the body presents, and you can easily find more examples for yourself.

Let us now look at the torso from a three-quarter view as given in Fig. 18.

You find here first: the superposition of one Pectoral over the other Pectoral; *i.e.* the Pectoral nearer to the eye than the other (2) which follows the receding plane of the upper mass of the torso, is outlined above this latter.

2. In the central part of the torso the mass of the Abdominal muscles (3) nearest to the eye stands out against the further ones (4) for the same reason.

3. The mass numbered 4 is relieved over the Oblique muscle numbered 5. The other Oblique, numbered 6 being more projecting than the abdominal muscles, is superposed on these. It is the same with the outline of the thorax; (7) its cartilaginous part stands out above the abdominal muscles, and so on.

You will have realised that this is one of the most important points in the study of relief. The few examples of superposition which I have demonstrated are the most accentuated ones, but you may continue them *ad infinitum*. Occasionally you find them with very delicate gradations, but having practised your eye by study, they will end by lying

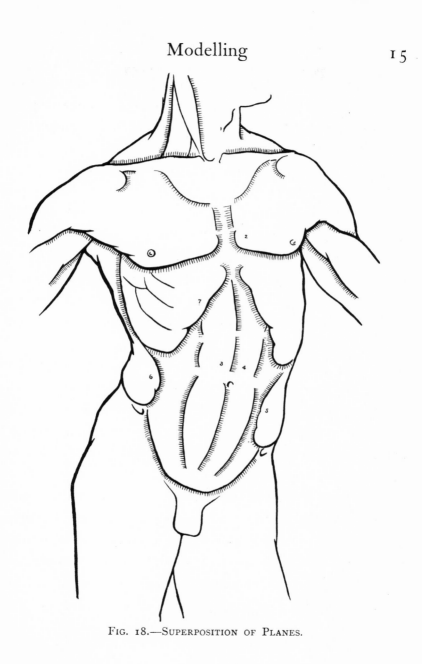

FIG. 18.—SUPERPOSITION OF PLANES.

quite clearly before you. The more you have made this principle your own, and applied it with all the conscientiousness that our profession demands, the more will you be able to appreciate its value.

Thus the first thing we have to look out for after the pose, is the relation of the large surfaces to each other, that is, their relative projections according to the view we have of the model.

These relative projections must be copied faithfully in your studies. At a later period, when your work has a decorative purpose, or when you do a composition in relief, you may dodge a little, but not in the elementary studies you are doing.

I am perfectly aware that to copy nature faithfully in relief as relative projection, does not often produce a good relief according to the laws of harmony, but regardless of these considerations, our studies from nature must be executed with perfect sincerity and great respect for the model.

When you are more advanced in the study of relief, and have quite mastered its principles, you may, even you must take some liberties to obtain the harmony of planes which a relief requires ; but this belongs to the domain of composition, of which I shall treat later on.

To return to our first study : Having with the wire-tool

(Fig. 10) cut the surfaces broadly, and sharply, you may perhaps lose the outlines, but do not be alarmed at that, for you will recover them more easily by the careful drawing of the planes they contain.

The large mass of more or less accentuated planes, each receiving the light differently, give not only a rich effect to the surface, but also suppleness to the form.

In this work of relief anatomical knowledge is necessary, but it does not play so important a part as in the figure in the round ; for what we are modelling is not the actual, real thing, only we have to do our best to suggest the effect of nature.

It would even be damaging to work much with a view to anatomy, for one might unconsciously fall into working in the same style as from the round ; one would be inclined to add to the projection and not only might one exceed the projection settled for the work, but also by attending only to the anatomy of the model, one would neglect the study of the superposition of planes, one would blend all the forms together and obtain again the doll-like effect. *See* Figs. 19, 20, 21 ; the difference only being, that this one would be round, instead of flat ; but there would be the same lack of suppleness in the contours.

On a round part the light glides and does not come to a stop, it determines no proportion and does not arrest the eye ; the latter too, sweeps over the whole form without being arrested by characteristic points of the whole.

Let the student gain this experience for himself. Sketch out any relief by strongly exaggerating the flat planes, in

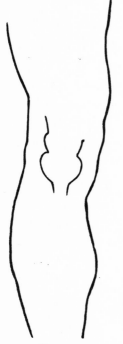

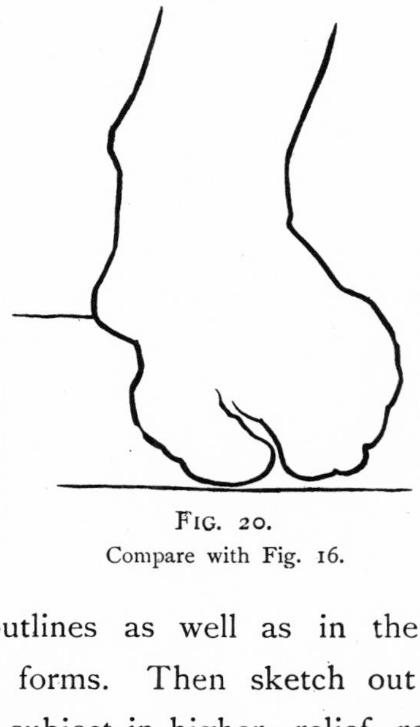

FIG. 20.
Compare with Fig. 16.

the outlines as well as in the interior forms. Then sketch out the same subject in higher relief, round the planes off and blend them in exaggerated fashion. Now place both these reliefs side by side at a good distance, and you will become aware of the difference in quality of the two. The one with flat planes will, so to speak, write down all the forms and fix their character,

FIG. 19.
Compare with Fig. 15.

Fig. 22.

because light as well as shadow will be held in place by the arresting angles; in the other one, on the contrary, the light will spread all over, and will consequently write down nothing; it will be vague and undecided all over.

After you have applied in your study all the above-mentioned rules and firmly drawn it, with perhaps a little

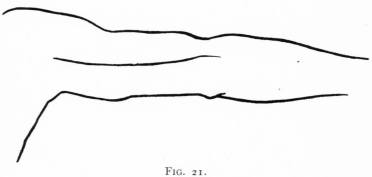

FIG. 21.
Compare with Fig. 17.

exaggeration, it will be easy to modify the latter, to take off its crudeness or hardness. You have only to let yourself be guided by your anatomical knowledge to give the right direction to the forms, just as you would do when modelling in the round. Fig. 22.

The study of relief must, even more than the study in the round, be done by colour. You must not work long under the same effect of light and shadow; you must frequently change the lighting, but be careful always to place your work and the model under the same effect.

As it is impossible to give in a relief of one inch thickness the same intensity in the dark shadows that you see in the model, you must make a scale of values. If the darkest shadow in the model has, figuratively speaking, an intensity of

TONE VALUE IN THE MODEL

COMPARATIVE TONE VALUE IN RELIEF

FIG. 23.

sixteen degrees, and if we cannot obtain more than four degrees of depth in our relief of one inch projection, all the secondary values must be taken in the same proportion, *i.e.* as 16 to 4. Fig. 23.

By changing the light you have the advantage of lighting up what was in shadow, and may then observe the richness

Fig. 24.

of planes which you did not notice when in shadow. And you can give the breadth of substance of nature to these planes, which might have appeared hollow to us whilst they were in shadow. Then, by turning again, and placing this part on which you have just worked in full light, you will observe other things and thus your work will progress. (Fig. 24.)

# CHAPTER II

In the study of drapery it is just as necessary to learn construction, as in the study of the head and figure, for of whatever material it is arranged, the construction of the folds is invariably the same.

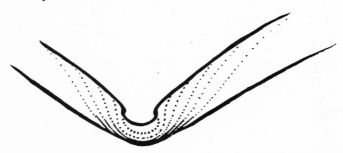

Fig. 25.—The Eye of the Fold, showing the Starting-point of the Planes.

Before trying an arrangement on the figure we must study a fold by itself.

All folds have a movement of surfaces or planes. This movement starts from a certain point and is constantly repeated. We may call it the anatomy of the fold.

One of its chief characteristics is, what in studio-slang we call, "the eye of the fold"; it is here that we find the starting-point of all the planes, as indicated in Fig. 25.

You will easily understand this, if you take a piece of clay and make an even round stick of it, about eight or nine inches long; imagine this to represent a fold falling vertically, of even thickness all its length.

Having pressed this stick of clay in the middle and turned it at a right angle (Fig. 26), you will find that the pressure in the centre has pushed the material out and formed a more prominent point than the surrounding

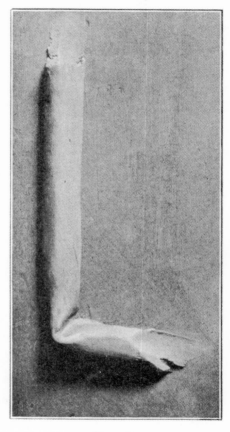

Fig. 26.

part; this is called the eye of the fold, and by an invariable rule, directly above this eye will be a projection. (Fig. 27.)

It is important to observe the direction of planes round this projecting point. (Fig. 28.)

Around the eye there is a rapid movement of planes, which gradually extends until it meets with a corresponding movement starting from another eye. (Figs. 28 and 29.)

This principle applies to any kind of drapery, although it is more or less accentuated in the different materials. In silk (Fig. 30), for instance, which is a rigid material, the eye

FIG. 27.—SHOWING PROJECTION OF THE EYE OF THE FOLD.

is more angular, the differences in the proportion of the fold are more marked than in any other material ; the background, or rather the interior of the folds, is generally larger, the drawing of the folds is less elegant, more broken up, giving rather a "baroque" effect. Employed in sculpture, this material may give a brilliant effect, but a slightly vulgar one ; however, as you may be called on to make a statue in modern costume, where silk is frequently employed, it is well to make a special study of silk folds, and by simplifying the lines and details, by treating the whole broadly, you may succeed in giving it a good sculptural effect. Modern Italian sculptors make a point of getting an exact representation of

FIG. 28.—SHOWING DIRECTION OF PLANES ROUND THE EYE OF THE FOLD.

this material, and the result is the vulgarity which characterises this school.

In velvet (Fig. 31) the projecting point about the eye is

more rounded.    In muslin (Fig. 32) the eye is less palpable,
the folds being softer.    This is the material which lends itself
best to sculpture; being light and transparent, it allows the
form underneath to be visible, though clothed; the proportions of the folds, which are as a rule small, make a good

FIG. 29.—DIAGRAM SHOWING MOVEMENT OF PLANES ROUND THE EYE OF
THE FOLD.

contrast to the breadth of the human form; they follow its
undulations and blend with it.    The Greeks employed muslin
more than anything else for draping the figures of women
and sometimes by way of contrast, to give more richness,
they combined it with another material that fell in larger

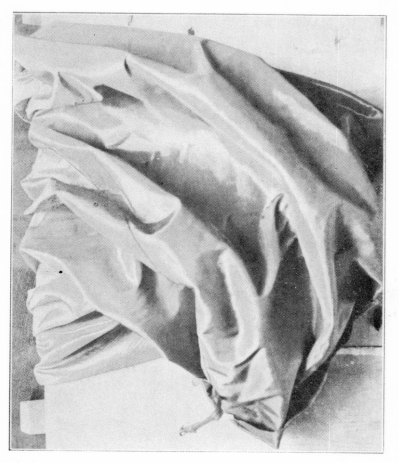

Drapery Arranged on a Board.

Fig. 30.—Silk.

Drapery Arranged on a Board.

Fig. 31.—Velvet.

Drapery Arranged on a Board.
Fig. 32.—Muslin.

Drapery Arranged on a Board.
Fig. 33.—Group of Folds Suitable for Copying.

folds. But, although less pronounced than in silk or linen, the principle mentioned above exists in muslin folds. Knowing this rule well, you can easily detect it notwithstanding all the accidental details which at first seem to conceal it.

You can have an exaggeration of this principle by trying to make a fold with a piece of oil cloth, and there you will easily observe it.

But I warn you against attempting to model a fold without having grasped this principle, for, I repeat, it is always the same, and every arrangement of drapery is a repetition of it in all the folds which compose it.

We must not forget, that, as in the figure or bust, or any other subject of sculpture, it is preferable to begin by laying on a small amount of clay, and to add to it gradually in order to obtain the quantity of the model we wish to represent. By putting on too much clay to begin with, you are compelled to cut and scrape off, and thus you entirely lose the freshness and expression of the model.

Now having well grasped the rule which I have been trying to explain, provide yourself with an even background of clay on a board, also with another board and fix both in a vertical position.

Arrange a group of folds of different forms (Fig. 33) on the second board and begin to copy the same from the front view. Lay the clay on in small rolls to indicate the drawing and the composition of the folds, as well as the exact proportion of distance from eye to eye. It is just these distances which—as in the construction of the bust or the figure—give you the characteristic likeness of the arrangement of drapery. See Fig. 34, photograph from the clay in the first stage.

After having indicated all the folds from the front-view, work on both sides from the profile, in order to establish the variety in the projections; then come back to the front-view and work from below.

Now you may begin to mark the projection above the eyes, and from these points indicate the movement of the planes or surfaces by exaggerating it. See Fig. 35, photograph from the clay in the second stage.

In progressing with your work, instead of seeing to the superficial part of the folds, it is preferable to finish the bottom or interior first, so as to avoid spoiling the exterior of your work.

Having most carefully finished the interior parts, you may go on to finish the projecting parts. This mode of proceeding will give suppleness to the work, and by joining the surfaces of the deep underparts to those of the projecting parts, you get a continuation of planes which will give restfulness and breadth to your work.

I strongly insist on this way of progressing, having often

Modelling Drapery on a Board.

Fig. 34.—First Stage.

Modelling Drapery on a Board.

Fig. 35.—Second Stage.

found that students are very careless about the interior parts, not only in draperies, but in every other work they do. There is a little difficulty about it, which seems to prevent them, a certain want of skill—not to call it laziness.

The moment when the student has grasped that it is the finishing of the interior parts which give suppleness to the outer face, or surface, he has made a great step in advance.

You may work indefinitely on the more visible parts, but if the inner depth is not finished with the greatest care, you will only produce an inert mass of folds.

In Nature what is hidden from sight is worked out as carefully as what is before our eyes—hence its grandeur of aspect. It is the same as in a head for the back part of the ears, the interior of the nostrils, &c. As I have already stated in the previous volume regarding this subject, it is impossible to obtain the supple aspect of either feature if the interior parts are not drawn and modelled first. And I must again and again impress on you, to finish the interior parts first, else you will never obtain a life-like effect.

I should like to draw your attention to the great care with which the drapery of Gothic figures is executed. If you look at the section of the folds, you will note that they are not a simple cut into the stone, but extend sideways underneath the projecting folds (see Fig. 36), so that the shadows produced by these deep-lying parts are not hard shadows, on

the contrary, often some light will get upon them and cause
a charmingly transparent shadow, from which the outer fold
is strongly detached. It
acts thus as a foil and gives
a rich effect, while at the
same time simple and chaste
in line and planes.

FIG. 36.—SECTION OF GOTHIC
DRAPERY.

Having finished the in-
terior parts and studied the
surfaces as far as line, proportion of length and comparative
width are concerned, and modelled the movement of the
planes, a few realistic details may be useful to interrupt the
hardness which the exaggeration of the planes may have
caused.

Here it is a question of taste to choose details which will
add life and force to the work, and to suppress others which
would be useless for this purpose and might only give an
effect of confusion.

In the same way as for the head and figure, you may at
this point work by colour. Try to put your drapery and
your own work in the same light, that is, under the same
effect of shadow and light and work by comparing the values
of shadows in the model and in your study. You will thus
obtain simplicity. (See Fig. 37, photograph from the clay in
the third stage, and Fig. 38.)

FIG. 37.

FIG. 38.—COPY IN CLAY OF FIG. 33.

# Modelling

The tools for modelling drapery are the same as for any other modelling. You will find a wire tool and a tool which has the shape of the thumb, as shown in Figs. 39 and 40, extremely useful for the ground. Besides these it will be necessary to have two brushes, a flat one and a round one; their size will depend on the size of your work. You will find them very helpful for cleaning the inner part of your folds, as they will allow you to reach more easily into the depth of the hidden parts than any other tool that I know of. They will particularly assist you to smooth the surface of these inner hollow portions.

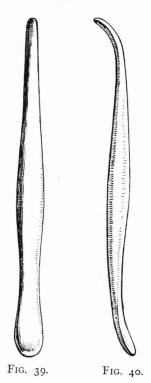

FIG. 39.        FIG. 40.

For the finishing stage of the drapery-study you ought to use softer clay; it will be more plastic or pliable than the foundation of the work, and render it easier to simplify exaggerated portions by spreading it lightly with the finger over them, without destroying the planes obtained before.

## THE ARRANGEMENT OF DRAPERY

DRAPERY is the generalisation of clothing. The garments which adapt themselves to climate, manners, and taste are called costume.

Antique art at its zenith always draped its figures, only in archaic period or in the period of Roman decadence do we find an imitation of costume.

In Greek .statuary male figures, apart from portraits, were rarely clothed. In bas-relief, which comes near painting, the Greek costume found its place, being so extremely simple, that it lent itself easily to sculpture.

The living model, draped and left undisturbed, gives us

at every turn excellent arrangements, but, in order to copy
these without alterations, one must work very quickly, as the
model can after all only sit for a limited time. And this
is a quality one acquires only in time, and after having previously studied drapery on a lay-figure or plaster cast, and
knowing well the principles and laws of the direction of folds
and their masses.

It behoves us therefore to make at first a study from or
after an immovable object which will allow us the necessary
time to comprehend the principles, which the Greeks have
taught us so well by their magnificent works, and which I
shall try to put before you.

Later on, when you are quite familiar with the subject,
it will be an excellent plan to make studies in this style
from the model (Fig. 41, 42, and 42A), rapid sketches where-
in you force yourself to give its spirit and reproduce the
large movement of the fold as well as the general character
of the model. But to begin with it needs a careful study
of the principles and reasons, which when well known, give
you the necessary skill to make studies from nature in small
proportions.

Although the arrangement of drapery on a figure may
be a matter of individual taste, there are certain canons which
you must know and follow.

Firstly: An arrangement of drapery must on no account

by false direction of folds hide the figure ; on the contrary, each fold, each detail of folds must contribute to explain the nude underneath by its movement, direction, and form. If this rule is not adhered to, the result will be a confused mass of lines without obvious reason or harmony.

Secondly : There must be a general direction, a chief or leading movement in the arrangement of the drapery, which the artist will select according to the pose of the figure and the decorative effect he wants to obtain.

For this sort of study it is a good thing for the student to begin with a simple arrangement on a plaster-cast ; then gradually go on to more complicated arrangements with different materials—for instance, a muslin tunic, and over this tunic a piece of flannel arranged in folds ; this will be an excellent practice in observing the different thickness of folds as well as their different treatment.

A plaster-statue that is to be draped should be covered with a solution of bees'-wax and turpentine. You may use the following recipe : Pour a pint of turpentine into a saucepan, take a piece of bees'-wax as big as an egg and shred it finely before putting it into the saucepan to dissolve. Place this saucepan on a gentle flame, or better still, lest it should catch fire, inside a larger pan filled with hot water, and let it melt, stirring it occasionally. When the wax has been reduced to a liquid state, dip a large brush into this mixture

FIG. 41.—TIME SKETCH FROM THE LIVING MODEL

Fig. 42.—Time Sketch from Life.

FIG. 42A.—TIME SKETCH FROM LIFE.

and paint the statue over with it, allowing it to dry quickly. If necessary, give it another coat of the mixture an hour later. For this second layer you must of course reduce the solution again to a liquid state, else the wax would lie too thick on the statue. This coat of wax and turpentine will prevent the statue from absorbing the moisture of the drapery, so that it does not dry before you have had time to make a serviceable arrangement of folds.

It is preferable to use a damp material for your first drapery studies, because the folds will adhere better to the statue than if they were dry, and you obtain by these means an exaggeration which will show up the principle more clearly.

Dip your material—and I would recommend a rather thick material at first, for instance, flannelette—into water and wring it out again, leaving enough moisture in it to make the folds fall well. Then cover the statue with this material and you will immediately observe that all the projecting points of the figure arrest the drapery and become starting-points for other folds. I now only mention this very important matter, but shall enlarge on it further on.

The first thing to do is to find a chief line, that is, the general direction of the fold or the mass of principal folds, which will, so to speak, be the line of expression ; for this fold, or mass of folds, must be directed according to the movement of the figure, and must contribute to its expression of action.   Fig. 43.

This chief line will divide the figure in unequal parts, and those parts will be filled by masses of folds.

Between each of these masses you must find some rest, that is some plain part, for these spaces of rest will give value to masses of folds, and will at the same time allow the forms of the figure to appear through.   Figs. 44 to 53.

You must avoid in the large masses to have the folds equal in size ; that would become monotonous.   A certain variety of volume in the folds will on the contrary cause more variety of shadow and light, and give at the same time more interest to the arrangement.   I am well aware that there are examples, for instance in Byzantine art, where the folds are generally parallel in direction and of equal size, but I do not think that you should follow their example in a study.

The most important rule for an arrangement of drapery is, that all the lines made by the folds should take their starting-point from the salient points of the nude ; all such salient points become centres of radiation for the folds.   See Figs. 45 to 53.

As in Architecture and Drawing, so in Sculpture, it is the salient points of the outline that determine the proportion and stamp its character on the work, so the lines of folds,

Drapery Arranged on Plaster Cast.

Fig. 43. — Chief Line of Drapery.

Drapery Arranged on Plaster Cast.
Fig. 44.--Complete Arrangement.

Drapery Arranged on Plaster Cast.

FIG. 45.—SIDE VIEW OF FIG. 44.

FIG. 46.—ARRANGEMENT OF DRAPERY ON THE LIVING MODEL.

FIG. 47.

A. Point of radiation of the folds.    B. Mass of folds.    C. Space of rest.

Fig. 49.

A. Point of radiation of the folds.      B. Mass of folds.      C. Space of rest.

Fig. 48.—Arrangement of Drapery on the Living Model.

FIG. 50.—ARRANGEMENT OF DRAPERY ON THE LIVING MODEL.

FIG. 51.

A. Point of radiation of the folds.    B. Mass of folds.    C. Space of rest.

FIG. 53.
A. Point of radiation of the folds.    B. Mass of folds.    C. Space of rest.

Fig. 52.--Arrangement of Drapery on the Living Model.

coming from different directions and blending with each other at the salient points of the nude, attract the eye of the spectator and guide it to the characteristic points. When you have these central points well established, the arrangement becomes strong and "clear," and the folds springing from there will complement and accentuate the figure in its action and proportion.

You will see by the diagram, Fig. 54, where the folds take a false direction of radiation, and by comparing it with Fig. 55, where the folds go to the one starting-point, how the former is wanting in harmony and construction.

It is not only the salient points of the nude figure which become starting points for the folds, but also the movements which raise a drapery. If the latter is carried over the arm, and you bend this arm, the folds will close up at the joint, and cause radiation. See Fig. 56.

Or if the drapery is grasped by the hand, the folds will group themselves in a very small space and spread out thence in their various directions. See Fig. 57.

Again, if a drapery is supported by a limb stretched in a more or less horizontal direction, its folds will be strewn over the limb without any radiation, as you see in Figs. 58 and 59 where the folds appear in an almost equal distance over the raised limb until they touch the knee, and there, the direction of the leg passing from the horizontal to

Fig. 54.—Drapery showing False Direction of Folds.

the vertical, with the knee projecting, radiation takes place.

You will also note in this same figure, that the background,

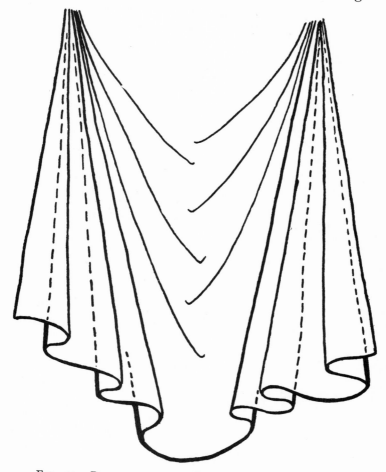

FIG. 55.—DRAPERY SHOWING RIGHT DIRECTION OF FOLDS.

or back-plane of a fold is generally larger than the fold itself; Fig. 59A, it is smoother and more even than the fold, it

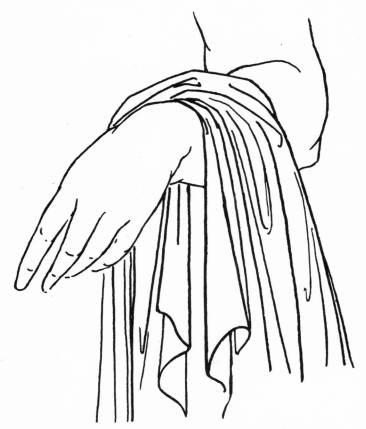

FIG. 56.—BENT ARM WITH RADIATION OF FOLDS.

appears lighter and brighter, so that it makes a strong foil for the fold, which appears almost like a half-tint on the

light background ; this pushes it forward, and gives relief
to the work without a great projection, it allows the folds

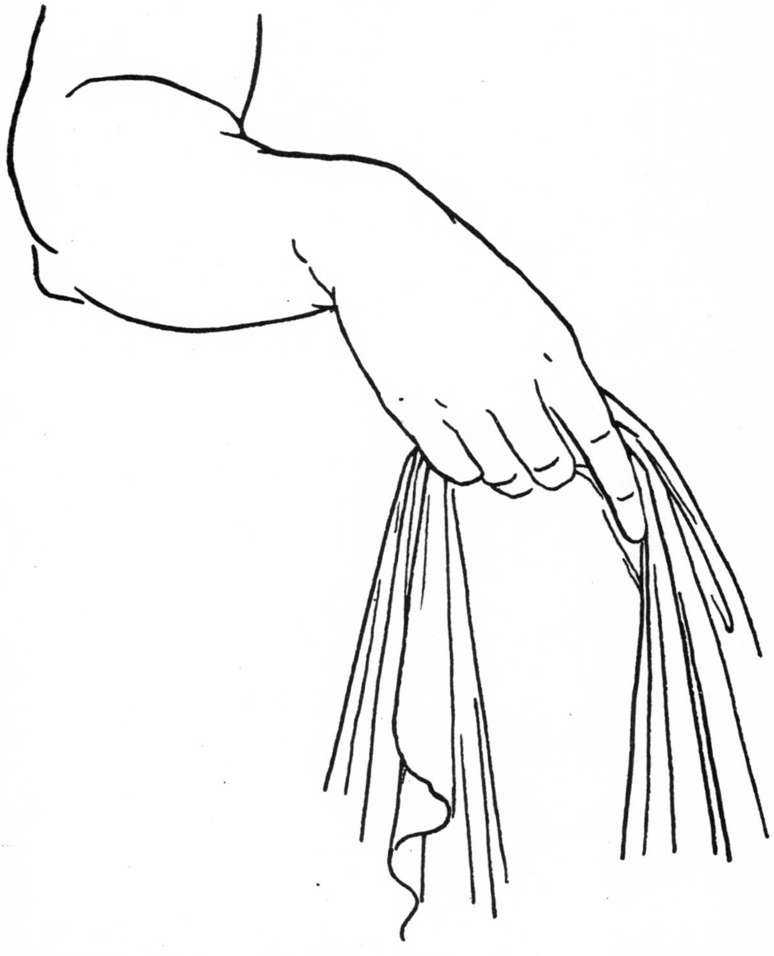

FIG. 57.—RADIATION OF DRAPERY WHEN GRASPED BY THE HAND.

FIG. 59.

× Point of radiation of the folds.　　o Parallelism of the folds.

FIG. 58.—VICTORY.  SHOWING PARALLELISM OF THE FOLDS ON THE THIGH
AND RADIATION FROM THE KNEE.

to follow the form of the nude and to give it force and
richness.

If you study the greatest masterpiece of draped Sculpture,
"the Fates" by Phidias, (see photograph of "the Fates."
Fig. 60) you will deduce these principles very plainly from
them. See Fig. 61 of a diagram after "the Fates."

When you have the chance of seeing a cast from this group,
or the original in the British Museum, I advise you to look up

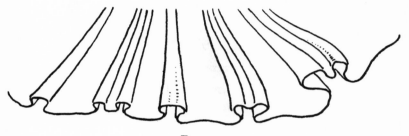

FIG. 59A.

into the folds from underneath. You will then observe another
principle : namely, that all the shadows cast by the folds will
draw the section of the nude ; these shadows follow completely
the graceful undulations of the figure and illustrate its form.

If on the other hand the shadows of the fold which touch
the nude were in a more or less straight, horizontal or vertical
line, the substantial force of the figure would disappear, and
although the statue is in the round, it would have the appearance of low-relief.

FIG. 61.

× Point of radiation.

Fig. 60.—The Fates.

Let us for instance take the example of a girdle placed underneath the bosom. If the line of the girdle were quite horizontal (see Fig. 62), the line would never suggest the roundness of the body. But if you exaggerate the round direction of this line (Fig. 63) by following as near as you

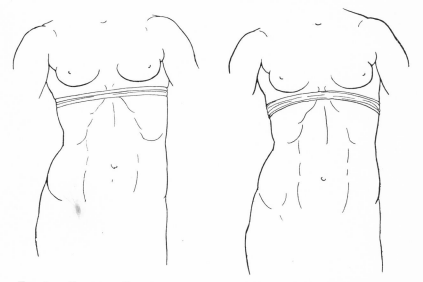

FIG. 62.—SHOWING GIRDLE IN A HORIZONTAL LINE.

FIG. 63.—GIRDLE FOLLOWING THE SECTION OF THE FIGURE.

can the section of the figure at this part, you will observe that the statue loses nothing of its roundness and consequent force.

All these rules you must learn in the beginning, but later on, your artistic feeling may and must take those liberties which your own ideas suggest ; but understand, that for all art-work, in order to take liberties you must first know the unalterable laws of nature, and then, if you want to accentuate here and there, in order to give strength and character to your work, you will not do it in haphazard fashion.

In the arrangement of drapery we come very near to the subject of composition, for the latter is more the result of feeling than calculation.

Your taste must dictate harmony and grace of line in the matter of folds. The expression which you want to obtain in a figure must guide you in the general movement of folds for their direction.

One of the most important points therefore is the harmonising of the lines of drapery with those of the figure ; however this, if carried too far, might become insipid and affected. Here it is that artistic feeling comes in. A discordant note thrown in with spirit and discretion may, by contrast, give value to the other lines. A great contrast in the direction of the lines of drapery with the movement of the figure may even accentuate this action. See the example in photograph, Figs. 64, 65, 66.

All folds which touch the nude must be what I would call discreet, but where the folds are away from the figure, you may take all the liberties which good taste will allow. See photograph of the figure of " Victory," Fig. 67.

FIG. 64.—ARRANGEMENT OF DRAPERY ON A PLASTER CAST, SHOWING CONTRAST OF THE LINE OF DRAPERY WITH THE MOVEMENT OF THE FIGURE.

FIG. 65.—SHOWING LINE OF CONTRAST OF FIG. 64.

In this figure you will note with how much care and delicacy this principle is carried out ; the folds adhere to the nude in following the model and the undulating curves of its forms, which are strong and well-rounded, and, notwithstanding, the figure looks and is perfectly clothed ; but the folds which float around this figure are treated with great liberty and an abundance of lights and shadows, some of them carved deep into the marble block, and yet simple in character, for the light glides so softly over them that you pass gradually to half-tint, and from half-tint to shadow without the shadows being absolutely black.  The treatment of this floating drapery makes a violent contrast with the sober effect which the drapery touching the figure produces, and thus they give value to each other.

In nearly all the best antique statues, those in the round and those in relief, you find a repetition of this treatment. Like everything instantaneous, floating draperies cause the sculptor great difficulty, and here he ought to be guided almost entirely by his artistic feeling, for these draperies become, as we might say, the frame for the figure ; they add to its movement, and even indicate the previous movement.

For a relief it is fairly easy to obtain a good *motif* of floating draperies by throwing a piece of linen on a background in the lines one wants (Fig. 68).  This means may

FIG. 66.—MAENAD: CHIMAIROPHONOS. SHOWING CONTRAST OF LINE OF
DRAPERY WITH THE MOVEMENT OF THE FIGURE.

FIG. 67.—VICTORY (NIKE) OF SAMOTHRAKE.

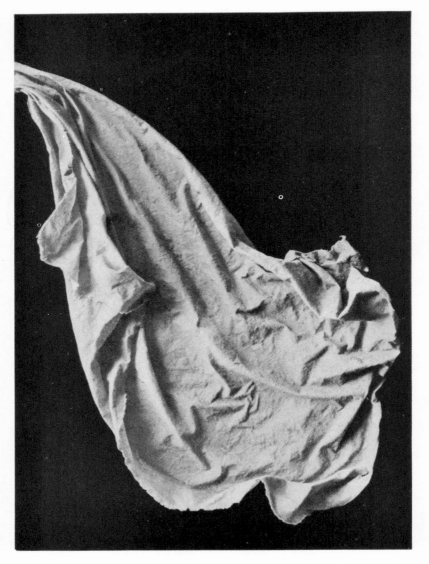

Fig. 68.—Flying Drapery Arranged on a Background.

also be employed for a figure in the round by giving in the execution a greater movement of planes than you obtain with the drapery arranged on a background.

In a floating drapery the principle of radiation of the folds must be still more emphasised, as you see in Fig. 69, where the folds grouped at the starting-point spread out below it,

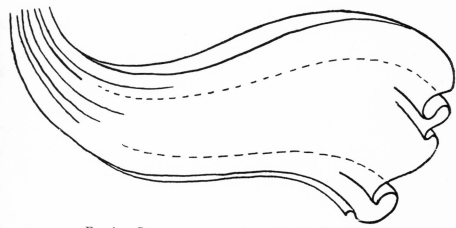

FIG. 69.—RADIATION OF FOLDS IN FLYING DRAPERY.

so as to suggest that the air swells and supports the material. Parallel folds could never render this effect so well, which fact you will at once realise when you compare the figures 69 and 70 with each other. See also Fig. 71.

If the character of the garment and the fineness of the material require small folds, they must be distributed in groups, so that several of these small folds form only a subordinate part of a large mass formed by a principal or leading fold.

The drapery ought to help us in explaining the action or expression of the figure-subject. If, for instance, the figure is floating in the air, the drapery ought to explain whether

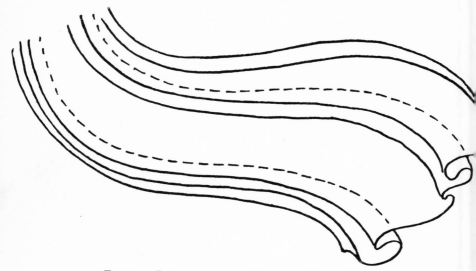

FIG. 70.—PARALLELISM OF FOLDS IN FLYING DRAPERY.

it is ascending or descending. If it is ascending, a column of upper air will weigh on the draperies; if it is descending, on the other hand, the air sustains them and holds them up.

The play of the draperies ought also to show whether the figure is in repose or in action, or, when the action has ceased, whether it was slow, quick, or violent. (Fig. 72.)

FIG. 71.—FLYING DRAPERY.

FIG. 72.—FLYING DRAPERY.

Fig. 73.—Example of Arrangement of Drapery on the Lay Figure.

In draping his figures the artist must not forget that the nude figure is the principal part, and that draperies are only accessories, destined to clothe it but not to hide it, and that they must on no account be the result of caprice or whim.

To avoid mistakes, the sculptor should model his figure in the nude before draping it ; without this precaution he would run the risk of going astray, and would add to or take off without noticing it from the proportion of certain parts of the body, especially of parts where outline and form are hidden under the folds.

The nude of a figure to be draped should be rather stout than thin, for the shadows cast by the folds cut the figure in several parts and make it always appear of lesser volume.

It will be easier for you to copy drapery by using a lay-figure (Fig. 73), or a sketch from the nude in wax, or a sketch in clay, modelled in the desired action and afterwards cast in plaster ; but you must always keep account of the fact that drapery so arranged cannot have the suppleness which it would have if arranged on the living model.

You often hear it said that drapery reveals the lay-figure when there is hardness in the folds ; you must therefore be very careful in the disposition of your drapery, and also take care that the execution should be *naïve* and not betray the lay-figure.

The genius of the antique conceived drapery as a *motif* of variety, an expression of gracefulness and refinement. In order to enhance the attraction of beauty, they surrounded it with mystery, but a mystery which was not impenetrable and which allowed you to divine the form underneath.

In your first studies of drapery arrangements, you must faithfully copy what you see in the model ; you can never be too honest and sincere in study. Sincerity will make you observe nature better than interpretation will, and the different observations which nature in its varied character suggests to you, will furnish your artistic mind and prevent you in the future from repeating yourself, and thus will give variety to your future works of art.

However, as no arrangement of drapery whether on lay-figure, or statue, or living model, will give us without fail exactly what we want for a work of art, you will have to choose what to suppress and what to amplify. But do not commit the mistake of thinking that you must modify from the beginning in the arrangement on the model whatever does not absolutely please you.

I have often experienced, that when I had copied as sincerely and literally as possible what was before my eyes and expected to have to make great changes to improve on the lay-figure, I found to my great surprise when the work was finished that there was very little, sometimes nothing, to

Fig. 74.—Arrangement of Drapery on a Plaster Cast.

FIG. 75.—THE NUDE PREPARATIONS FOR COPYING FIG. 74.

FIG. 76.—FIRST STAGE, SHOWING CHIEF LINES OF DRAPERY.

Fig. 77.—Second Stage.

Fig. 78.—Third Stage.

change. But on the contrary, if you begin with suppressing in one place and adding in another, the result will be that none of your folds would agree and harmonise, for in the nature of folds one fold is the sequence of another. By proceeding thus you would have to make constant changes, and the model on the lay-figure would not be of any use or help to you.

Let us never forget that nature demands above all things to be respected. That will save us discouragement and sorrow ; our faith in nature gives us confidence and strength to struggle on. True courage and boldness as we admire it in the greatest artists can only be born from the feelings which study has developed. False courage, the conceit and self-consciousness of ignorance, is the most regrettable, most dangerous vice for an artist. It radically stops all development and progress. Modesty, the inclination for *naïve* research are, on the contrary, the most precious qualities in a beginner. He will get bolder in proportion as he understands better and has his artistic feeling more strongly developed. Such courage will not degenerate into vainglorious self-conceit.

MODELLING FROM AN ARRANGEMENT OF DRAPERY ON A
PLASTER CAST.

Figs. 74–78 show the various stages of the work.

Obverse.

ISOTTA ATTI DA RIMINI (FOURTH WIFE OF SIGISMONDO PANDOLFO MALATESTA).

BY MATTEO DE PASTI OF VERONA. 1446.

Reverse.

AN ELEPHANT.

BY MATTEO DE PASTI OF VERONA. 1446.

# MEDALS

## CAMEOS AND INTAGLIOS

Connected with Low-Relief Sculpture is Glyptic Art, that is, the art of graving in relief or hollowing out hard stones.

If we suppose that all historic monuments of Architecture, Sculpture, and Literature had been destroyed, that the remembrance of the Old World had been completely effaced from the memory of Man, and that in this shipwreck or deluge of human knowledge nothing had been saved but a collection of engraved stones, coins, and medals, the discovery of this treasure-trove might suffice perhaps to rebuild and recompose the history of the vanished monuments and time. These engravings on metal and hard stones are indeed as books printed on them ; they give speaking descriptions ; men and objects are outlined on them by tangible representations ; their inscriptions are concise, but lucid, eloquent, and definite.

The word Glyptics signifies engraving, and is in particular applied to hard stones, that is, gems, rock-crystal, precious and semi-precious stones. We distinguish Intaglios, *i.e.* gems, where the design is hollowed out, and Cameos, where the design is carved in relief.

It is through these cameos and intaglios that we know what the master-pieces of Ancient Sculpture were like, as they frequently contained low-relief copies of famous works and were splendidly executed by the Greeks and Romans —I remind you here of the *Maenad* of Scopas in the British Museum Gem-room and the *Philoctetes* by Pythagoras in the Berlin Museum—and again in the Renaissance times by artists of the northern nations.

The originals for the cameos as well as for the intaglios are modelled in wax, and the stone is afterwards engraved by means of iron tools ending in a small disc or a ball, which is moistened with oil and diamond-dust. The other end of the tool is fixed to a diminutive lathe, and the worker's hand and eye are used to guide and direct the tool.

But this is a branch of art which has declined in our times, as there is little demand for artistic modern cameos.

## MEDALS

The art which concerns us more nearly is that of medal-engraving.

A medal is a piece of metal like a coin, but whilst coins bear the impression of a sovereign state or its ruler, and are circulated as means of exchange or money, medals are never circulated as such, but are struck in celebration or remembrance of persons or events, and are bestowed as a mark of distinction by sovereigns or authorities.

A medal has two sides, the face or obverse, so named because it generally bears a head, and the back or reverse, which bears some relief or simply an inscription. Its engraving demands a laconic, concentrated style, and restricts the artist to give only what is essential and indispensable of the forms of his model.

The medallist has the choice of several styles of work : he can carve his figure in relief on a steel puncheon, and take from this relief the hollow mould or matrix into which the medal is struck, or he can directly hollow the mould out in steel and use this as matrix for the impressions of the medal—and this is the method which was formerly most in use—or he can have his model cast and work it up by hand.

Of late years the art of engraving medals and coins has gone down. Mechanical processes are employed, and the result is mediocrity. Medallists are often content to make their model four times as large as the proportion which the medal is to have, cast it in plaster and cast-iron, and have it reduced by machine to the desired size.

This is a very undesirable proceeding for figure-subjects on a medal, for the figures which are conceived in the large proportion of the model come near the relative proportion of nature which produces a petty effect in a medal. You will have observed in all antique medals or cameos, that the extremities of the figures are comparatively strong and large, that you are struck at once with the head and its character, the hand and its expression, that the personage stands well on his feet and retains thus in its small size a good balance and a grand air.

If you happen to make the proportions of the head and limbs exactly comparative to those of nature, which is generally done when first making a model on a large scale, after reduction it will appear like a rope-dancer or marionette, and will consequently lack force and nobility of aspect.

So you must learn the artifices or tricks which cause this branch of art to be not a simple imitation of nature, nor a mathematical reduction of objects, but a proud interpretation which prevents the artist from falling into cold servility.

The impression of any image or sign on a medal is called " type." The use of this word is neither indifferent or accidental. The very word indicates the principal quality required in a figure graven on gold, silver, or bronze : you must imprint on it, above all, the typical character of life—in other words, you must idealise it by comprehensive generic accents of life, as you must to a certain extent do in all works of sculpture, but more than ever in a medal.

In the most ancient medals the type is not yet the human head, but an inanimate object or a symbolical animal.

In the fourth century B.C. the face of the medal loses its allegorical character ; instead of local divinities it represents portraits, frankly resembling—I remind you of the medals bearing the portraits of Alexander and Antiochus. However, the reverse of the medal, which yields to the engraver's invention an open field, retains still a symbolical treatment of the nature and history of the country. If they have not a religious significance, the representations are in a way heraldic ; some are the arms of the people or the cities. Thus the reverse is in divers ways a more or less ingenious emblem which gives the mind something to understand or to guess at.

The laws of Numismatics, so marvellously written and laid down in Greek medals, and still well known and understood by the Romans, were lost awhile in the Middle Ages, the coins of which present a barbaric severity. Attempts to revive the art, like that of the Hohenstauffen emperor, Frederic II., who had his gold coins engraved after the pattern of antique coins, remain isolated, and it is reserved to the Masters of Italian Renaissance in the fourteenth and fifteenth centuries, above all to the genius of Vittore Pisano (who died in 1451), to revive the art of the medallist and bring it to rare perfection. Even in going nearer to nature he interprets it in masterly fashion by the character of the heads, which, even if you see them but once, make a lasting impression, so that you cannot forget them. They are no longer ideal figures, but living, speaking men, freely sculptured personalities, which stand out from the rest of humanity in history.

In the sixteenth century German goldsmiths and engravers distinguished themselves in engraving medals after designs of great painters. Albrecht Duerer is said to have himself executed three of his many drawings for medals.

In the seventeenth century Georges Dupré (who died in

1643) flourished in France (medal of the Doge Marcantonio Memmo), Fig. 79. His medals express not only the bodily and moral physiognomy of the individual, but seem to palpitate

Obverse.

FIG. 79 —MARCANTONIO MEMMO, DOGE OF VENICE (b. 1556, Doge 1612, d. 1615).

BY GEORGES DUPRÉ.

with life—the typical gives way to the realistic portrait. Although of high merit, his work is inferior to that of Vittore

COIN BY PISTRUCCI.

Pisano. A good many other medallists are found at this time among French artists, and the art-branch is considered so important that Louis XIV. founded the "Académie des Inscriptions," whose sole task was to provide inscriptions in classical Latin in the correct official style.

The modern inferiority of this art, and in particular of the numismatic branch—here I wish to except the fine representation of St. George and the dragon on some of our gold and silver coinage by Pistrucci—is almost entirely due to the previously described method of working, and the mechanical reduction of a model conceived in a different proportion. An unconscious, brutal machine, of blind obedience and mathematical monotony, has been substituted for the fibre of the artist's hand, the will of his soul.

Besides, in our coinage, struck on a flat disc, the relief must be even everywhere ; the thickness or depth of the type is kept exactly to the level of the borders, so that the coins may be piled up. Such necessity is not imposed on the engraver of medals, which, not being made for bankers and money-changers, may at least retain degrees in the relief and keep free from those exigencies in which the beautiful is sacrificed to the useful.

Study the beautiful Greek (Fig. 80) and Roman medals, as well as those of the Renaissance, especially Pisano's. These masterpieces will reveal their secrets to you and prove to

LYSIMACHUS.          PHILIP ARIDAEUS.

SYRIA, B.C. 145-142.

LOCRI OPUNTI.

FIG. 80.—GREEK MEDALS.

you more than any other examples that greatness is independent of dimensions, for greatness is a quality of the mind.

In any branch of sculpture the treatment is different for different proportions, and this is more especially the case with medals; the smaller they are the more need for simplifying the working. The Greeks understood this better than anybody else, and Pisano after them.

If you look at any Greek statuette of the good time, it strikes you as a whole by its grand aspect, and you do not take heed of its proportion, because it impresses you in the same way as a life-size work would. Nowadays, details, as numerous as they are useless, take away from the largeness of the work, and the public rejoices in this photographic sculpture, and says : " How beautifully done," where they ought to say : " How petty!" " How trivial!"

If you model your medal at once in the actual size, you will certainly make every touch in the scale of its general proportion, and will not feel the desire to overload it with wrinkles, crow's-feet, and details of hair; large planes will receive the light, and a few touches on them will give an air of fineness without looking poor.

A medal ought always to be treated broadly, but to model with breadth does not mean that you should carry this to boldness or insolence, as is so often done in these days—

fortunately more in painting than in sculpture. The medal
ought to show style more strongly than work on a larger

Obverse.

Fig. 81.—Leonello d'Este, Lord of Ferrara (b. 1407, lord, 1444,
d. 1450).

By Vittore Pisano of Verona (b. 1380, d. 1456).

scale. By style I mean simplified truth, divested of all
insignificant detail, in fact the typical aspect. There is nothing
more difficult than to get hold of intelligent life. You cannot

seize it by a literal imitation. If that were sufficient the photographer would be the best portrayer—and you know how

Reverse.

FIG. 81.— TWO NUDE MALE FIGURES BEARING BASKETS OF OLIVE BRANCHES ON THEIR HEADS.

BY VITTORE PISANO OF VERONA.

deceptive the infallible truth of the photographer's portrait is. An artist gifted with a soul can draw forth a soul.

Before a feeling and thinking being you must feel and

Obverse.

FIG. 82.—SIGISMONDO PANDOLFO MALATESTA, LORD OF RIMINI (b. 1417, lord, 1432, d. 1468).

BY MATTEO DE PASTI OF VERONA. 1446.

think yourself, consequently you must choose everything : the attitude, the lines of the dress, and even the proportion of the background, which is capable of making the head look smaller or larger.

If the person is tall, it will be well to make the crown

Reverse.

FIG. 82.—THE CASTLE OF RIMINI.

BY MATTEO DE PASTI OF VERONA. 1446.

of the head almost touch the upper border of the circle of the medal ; if the person is small, a certain distance left above the head will clearly indicate this fact.

In the interpretation of nature which the medal requires, the artist must work with spirit.  By spirit I understand not only the aptitude of seizing delicate degrees and making them stand forth by co-ordinating or contrasting them, but also the talent of perceiving the essential qualities which go to make a face and whatever there is characteristic and expressive in it.

This spirit shows to a marvellous extent in Vittore Pisano's work. His medal of " Leonellus Marchio Estensis " (Fig. 81) is in truth a surprisingly admirable portrait ; so is the Malatesta by Matteo Pasti (Fig. 82) ; you see there in indelible lines an individuality which you could not possibly mix up with any other—it is full of style, because it is the typical personification of a man with that peculiar character.

### EXECUTION

Before beginning a medal I advise you to make a life-size drawing of your model in order to study the proportions, the details, and the movement of the forms. This drawing should be sincere and faithful without attempting any interpretation. You can thus in the first sitting observe the carriage of the sitter, the pose of the head, you can analyse and familiarise yourself with all his other characteristics.

The best proportion for a medal is a diameter of from two to four inches, such as the masters of the Renaissance adopted. In a larger size the portrait loses the necessary concentration, the eye cannot so quickly seize its general character, and it comes near the proportion of the medallion.

FIG. 83.—PREPARATION IN CLAY.

On an even slate stick some modelling-wax, as thick as the projection of your medal is to be—(see Fig. 83)—without troubling about detail, beyond forming a rounded mass, diminishing in thickness at the outlines and giving in very low relief the idea of a section of a head. This will help to give the appearance of substance and solidity to the head. If you begin by making the forehead, then the nose, mouth, &c., there will be a want of homogeneity and unity in the general plan. The principle is the same which I have expounded in the chapter on Relief from Nature.

Of course you must at once give to this mass the pose of the head and the direction and planes of the shoulders,— if there are any shoulders. After that you hollow out the eye, project the nose and place the ear, which is generally parallel to the space containing nose and eye ; then from behind the ear draw the outline of the jaw to the chin and from the nose trace the profile line of the upper and lower lip to the chin. On this line draw the line of the mouth, indicate its corners and the outlines of the lips, then the forehead and outline of the head, the neck, and so on.

So far you should have worked with the light falling on the back of the model's head, so that the profile throws a cast shadow on the background. You will find it easier to draw broadly and you can better judge of the drawing and of the proportions, than if the light fell on the profile of the face.

Having thus placed the features, there follows the working of the planes, which should be done as broadly as possible, at decided angles which will allow you to test whether their direction is exact. (Fig. 84.)

And now you must change your light continually. I go
so far as to say, take the medal in your hand and follow

Fig. 84.—Indication of Features and Planes.

your model about the studio, so that you get a perpetual
change and yet have the same effect of light and shade on
your work as on your model.

Examine also from the front-view the relation between

the projections of the different parts, as, for instance, the relation of the forehead to the cheekbone, to the jaw and neck, the projection of the eye compared to the nostril, the relation of the latter to the mouth and chin, the cheek to the ear, and so on.

You must keep a strict eye on these relations, so as to bring them into harmony and into the general scale of the medal. I repeat that you cannot change the light too often, for if you work too long under one effect, the likeness obtained under this will disappear under another effect, and what appeared to be neatly drawn will look confused.

It requires very attentive, precise, and careful work before a medal can pass the examination and resemble the model under all effects of light.

In progressing with your work you must also be very cautious not to lose its general substance by hollowing out certain parts, or by allotting too much projection to others, and thus losing the foundation-plane.

The superposition of planes must be executed in the wax with great precision, it may even be pushed to hardness; you must verify them in every possible effect. In short, everything must be precise and sharp; nothing must be left to accident, there must be no jugglery with artful touches. In the plaster it will be easy to simplify and soften.

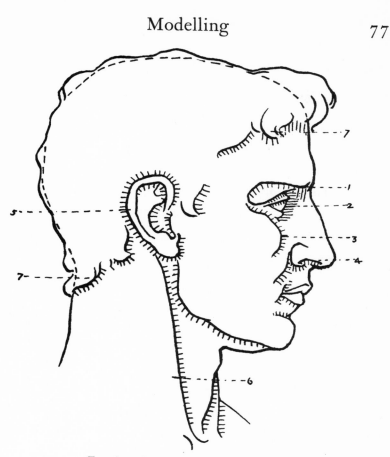

Fig. 85.—Superposition of Planes.

The principal superpositions of planes are:

1. The forehead over the eyebrow.
2. The eye over the nose.
3. The cheek over the eye, nose, chin, and neck.
4. The wing of the nose over the upper lip.

5. The ear over the posterior part of the cranium.

6. The sterno-cleido-mastoid muscle over the profile of the neck.

7. The hair over the whole of the upper part of the face and over the posterior part of the neck, &c.   (Fig. 85.)

When you have pushed your work in the wax as far as the material will allow, that is, if everything is well in place, the characteristic attitude and resemblance obtained, by decided drawing, the planes strongly defined, you may proceed to the casting in plaster of your medal.

With a soft brush wipe a little oil over the wax model and the slate background ; then mix your plaster—not too thick though—and throw a spoonful on the wax, blowing it about, so that it enters into all the hollow parts and makes a slight covering over the whole ; when it is settling add more plaster, to about the thickness of one inch.   Be careful to cover enough of the slate, so as to leave a good space all round the head, in order to have enough material to cut the background out of.

After about twenty-five minutes, or when the plaster begins to feel hot, you may remove the mould from the slate.   For this purpose place the slate with what is on it under water for two minutes, and then push a fine chisel underneath the plaster, use it as a lever, and raise the mould, which will readily come off the oiled wax.

You have by these means obtained a mould (Fig. 86) in which you can work and improve your medal to a degree which can only with difficulty be obtained in wax.    Suppose

FIG. 86.—MOULD FROM FIG. 84 RETOUCHED.

any of the forms, say the cheek, lacks roundness and rich- ness, it is easy to attain that effect by gently hollowing with a rounded tool this form, which was convex in the wax and is concave in the mould.    You must bear in mind that the amount which you take from the mould will add to the projection in the proof.

With fine and rounded tools you may thus go over all the parts of the medal which you wish to raise in relief.

In order to keep account of what you are doing, squeeze from time to time a piece of wax or clay into the mould over the parts on which you have been working, and you will at once see the effect in projection.

At first you will find some difficulty in knowing what you have done in the mould, as well as what you are able to do in it. It is an extremely rapid means of advancing your medal and giving freshness and brilliance to the forms. I advise you to practise it until you have well mastered its uses and advantages.

The difficulty of this method of working is greatly lessened by throwing a strong light from the side on the mould, so that you get violent shadows in the hollow, then screw up your eyes, and after having looked at it for a few instants you will see it in projection, and this impression will last some time, so that it is occasionally difficult to see it again as concave, and you work as if it were really in projection.

Another advantage of this system is, that—the hollow parts in the wax jutting out in the mould—you can finish them and clean them up more easily, round them off when necessary. This will prove a good quality in the cast, for the interiors will appear finished without having the hardness which tool-marks in the wax always cause, and there will be a continuity in the modelling, a gentle blending of surfaces with interior parts, in fact it will greatly assist in giving the quality of unity and harmony.

After having worked in this way all over the medal, it is well to take a wax squeeze of the whole medal, in order to see if it will be well to go on working in the mould or better to continue the work in relief.

If the work answers to your expectation, you take a proof in plaster. The first thing to do is to soap the mould with boiled soap : put half a pint of boiling water in a saucepan and add a good tablespoonful of black soft soap of unadulterated quality to it. Let this boil, and stir it until it is quite dissolved ; when cold, keep it in a corked bottle. I strongly recommend you to use no other preparation, as unless the soap is boiled, there will be unevennesses on the cast, for soft soap never gets quite dissolved when put on with cold water. Nor would I advise you to use hard soap by rubbing a wet brush on it and paint the mould with the froth ; this will cause an undesirable thickness in the mould and corresponding bluntness in the proof.

You may use the boiled soap hot or cold, it matters not which, only it must be liquid, and should it be too thick, add some boiling water to thin it.

The mould is then completely filled with this liquid soap and left with it for a few minutes ; then the liquid is poured off, and after having given it some more time to absorb the soap left on its surface, you remove with a soft brush whatever traces of soap are left in the hollows, and let it lie flat till the surface appears dry ; that will be in about 10 minutes' time. Now take four or five drops of olive oil in the hollow of your hand, and rub a thoroughly dry, soft brush on it, so that its hairs just get moistened at the extremities. If it should have imbibed too much oil and show diminutive drops at the ends, you must wipe them off on a clean linen rag. Wipe this brush gently over the surface of the soaped mould until you perceive a diffused sheen on the upper face of the plaster. After this place the mould in a vessel and cover it up with clean water, and leave it there until it cannot absorb any more water. This will take about three-quarters of an hour if the mould was quite dry.

If you do not use this precaution, you will have small holes in your cast which are caused through the dryness of the mould tending to absorb moisture from the cast and leaving air-bubbles in its place. When the mould is quite saturated with water, take it out of the pail and blow the large drops of water off ; it does not matter if a few small drops remain, as they will assist the plaster to run in the mould when you cast the proof. When everything is ready and a clay-band put round the mould to keep the plaster up, you mix the plaster very evenly. Then proceed as before, *i.e.* blow the first layer all over the surface to make it go into all the deep parts—you may even assist the process with a damp brush—and when it gains consistency, fill it up with plaster to a depth of one-half to three-quarters of an inch. It is preferable to make these early moulds and proofs rather thick. Allow the cast to set for about half-an-hour and then plunge it for a few minutes into water. This will assist the process of detaching the one from the other, for which you push a very slender blade between mould and proof. By gently pressing they will separate. If there should be any difficulty, you put the whole back into the water and manipulate the blade so that the water will glide between the two surfaces. Of course, these directions apply only to work which will draw off in one piece, where there is no undercutting.

A few minutes after you have drawn the cast off, and whilst the plaster is quite fresh, you can work on it with advantage by wrapping a fine linen or lawn rag over your finger, and modelling gently over the surface of the medal, as if you were modelling it in clay. This will blend and simplify the planes. You resume then the working from the model in the same way as you worked in the wax, correct and define the outlines, the superposition of planes, in short, do everything which can lend aid to accentuating the character ; you may also slightly indicate the direction of the hair.

At this stage it will be well to settle the circle of the medal. By means of a pair of compasses you strike a circle on the background, using as a centre the ear or a point near it ; from the same centre you strike two circles within the first, the distance between them depending on the size of the lettering for your inscription. Draw the inscription in place with a very hard pencil, which will slightly enter in the plaster, so that it will appear raised in the next mould (Fig. 87).

You take this next mould in the same way that I described for the first, but soap and oil your proof before putting it in water. When the second mould is ready, work on it or in it as in the first. The indication of the hair, moustache, and beard that you have made on the first proof will be in relief on the mould, and you can now dig them out with a tool according to the projection you wish them to have. Touch up the parts which seemed too flat in the cast by gently digging into the mould ; in short, repeat the operation that you pursued on the first mould in such a way that you advance your work with fineness and precision.

The letters standing out in the mould (Fig. 88) will also have to be incised (Fig. 89), so that they will be raised above the background in the next proof.

When you have done all you can in the second mould,

FIG. 87.—CAST FROM FIG. 86 RETOUCHED, AND INDICATION OF LETTERS.

take a fresh proof on which you continue your study in detail. You will always find it useful to wrap a rag round your finger when modelling over a fresh proof, to reduce and soften projections, for instance, of the hair or beard, or of the letters. By rubbing the latter with the rag when they are too high, you obtain much better quality than by using a tool to work them down. (Fig. 90.)

I should like to hint with regard to the hair that it is just as well to put too many details in the mould, as long as they are correct in their direction, because it is so easy

FIG. 88.—MOULD OF FIG. 87 WITH LETTERS IN PROJECTION.

to rub them down with the rag until there is hardly anything left to show of them but the planes, which will suggest the fineness of hair with the slight indications that are left.

If your medal has to be very small, say only one and a

half inches in diameter, and also very flat, it is preferable—
after having made a large drawing and perhaps modelled it
first in the larger size—to work it directly on the plaster to

FIG. 89.—LETTERING INCISED AND FACE AND HAIR RETOUCHED.

the required size. You take for this purpose a small
previously prepared plaque of plaster, thoroughly dry, and
draw the outline of the head and neck sharply on it in the
actual size you want, plunge it in water to soften the plaster,

FIG. 90.—CAST OF FIG. 89 RETOUCHED.

and when sufficiently soft to yield to a knife, cut it down
outside the drawn contour to the background, until you have
left enough relief for the head. When your background is
tolerably level, you begin to work on the plaster in the
same way as on the wax; the plaster being of firmer
substance, you can at once arrive at greater precision than
in the wax. When you have done all you can on the

plaque, take a mould of it, with the usual preliminaries of soaping and oiling, and in this mould you relieve the parts that are too flat, and work exactly as I have described it for the previous work.

As it is rather difficult, when you cut the plaster down round the head, to get a perfectly even background, and entirely in the same plane, the first mould gives you an opportunity

FIG. 91.—ROUGH SKETCH OF COMPOSITION.

FIG. 92.—SKETCH IN CLAY.

to remedy this defect. Take a sheet of fine sand-paper and lay it flat on a table or any perfectly level board, and then rub the face of the mould lightly on it, taking care to hold it quite horizontally, until the surface of the background is absolutely flat. Of course, the head being hollow, you do not run any risk of injuring it by this proceeding.

If you have to represent a draped figure, you must make

FIG. 93.—MOULD OF FIG. 92.

your composition first on a larger scale (Fig. 91), then make a study of it in drawing from nature, so that you are quite sure what you want to obtain in the medal.

Suppose this figure is to be on the reverse of a medal of three inches diameter. You trace on a slate a circle of this dimension, within which you sketch in clay the nude figure, at first in fairly flat projection. (Fig. 92.) Then you find the planes and contrasts as in the study of a relief, when you have the pose, the proportions, and the intended effect of surfaces. Take care to make the nude rather full,

Fig. 94.—Cast from Mould, Fig. 93, worked upon.

so that you have afterwards in the plaster sufficient material to draw the contours without making the figure poor and lean. The nude of a figure that is to be draped should be of rather comfortable proportions, particularly when it is for a small size, such as a medal.

Arrived at this stage, you must take a first mould, on

FIG. 95.—CAST WITH OUTLINE OF DRAPERY INCISED.

which you work in the same way as for a head. (Fig. 93.) Then take a proof in plaster, on which you draw and model the nude figure more correctly. (Fig. 94.) When you have finished it, take a very hard and finely-sharpened lead-pencil

FIG. 96.—MOULD OF FIG. 95, HAVING OUTLINE OF DRAPERY IN PROJECTION.

and draw upon the nude figure the folds after the study from nature, press gently on the pencil so that these directions for folds will be slightly incised on the plaster (Fig. 95); then make a second mould in which the fold indications will appear slightly raised (Fig. 96); hollow or dig them out to the depth that is necessary for the projection that you desire in the proof. (Fig. 97.) Take from time to time a squeeze

Fig. 97.—Mould of Fig. 95, with Drapery Engraved and Finished.

in wax to see how you are going on. If some part should have been graved too deep, you can easily work it down in the proof.

When you can no longer see in the mould what you are doing, draw a proof, on which you do all you possibly can by taking off (Fig. 98), drawing, and modelling, and if you find that in some part the relief is too flat, or the folds too

poor, you make a third, even a fourth mould, and go on
working in the same way.　Never be afraid of making several
moulds—I have sometimes taken as many as twelve moulds

FIG. 98.—CAST OF FIG. 97 RETOUCHED.

for a medal of this style, and found that after all that was
the quickest and surest way of advancing the work.　After
some practice you even arrive at engraving a medal or a
figure hollow into the plaster without any previous modelling

in wax, I mean starting with making the mould. Although this is somewhat difficult, I hold it to be no more so than modelling a draped figure direct entirely in wax, and you get a very good result. An object of small dimensions can always be worked in this way with advantage.

MEDAL BY THE AUTHOR.

# COMPOSITION

Of all art-subjects the most difficult and delicate to treat is Composition, for it cannot, properly speaking, be taught. In approaching this subject the teacher must use special diplomacy towards the student in order to suggest, rather than to impose on him, those modifications which will make him advance.

Here, more than in anything else, the master should become the physician of his pupil by pointing out to him what is suitable for his particular temperament.

Before saying anything to the student about the correction of his composition the master should try to assimilate the ideas which the student seeks to express. He should put himself in his place and become one with his pupil, and then with his riper experience continue the work by developing it and strengthening it, but respecting as much as possible the original conception. For a master to impose on his pupil his own conception of a subject is entirely contrary to the rules of artistic teaching ; in such a case the hand of the

Fig. 99.—Zeus Group from the Large Frieze of the Altar of Pergamon.

FIG. 100.—ATHENA GROUP FROM THE LARGE FRIEZE OF THE ALTAR OF PERGAMON.

student becomes merely the instrument of the master's brain, and he never acquires the needful strength of conviction to produce a work of individual quality. The only result is to make the student lose all interest in pursuing and perfecting his own conception. And yet this is just what the master ought to assist him in, by speaking to him of the masterpieces of old, and by using all possible means that will help him to give expression to his own thoughts and sentiments.

There is no positive law for composition ; still, there are some generally accepted " conventions " which the student will be glad to know without being put forward as absolute rules like the laws of the Medes and Persians.

These few rules are based on observations drawn from the works of various masters of different epochs ; but no master resembles another, nor one epoch of time another, and yet there are splendid works in almost all.

What would be the result if composition were taught like mathematics ? The training of people, who would all think and work in the same way, and who would have a ready prescription for every case. This is, perhaps, what one hears so often talked about as " a school." " This artist has founded a school by his teaching."

Is that a desirable result ? No, it is a most unfortunate result for Art, as by subjecting it to a fixed routine it kills the artistic germ which each individual may possess.

That is why positive lectures on composition are very dangerous; I mean those which lay down absolute laws, for, strange to say, the most interesting works of art are always those which have escaped and avoided those laws. Imagine a lecture (and I have often had the misfortune to be present at such an one) before fifty students, where it is affirmed that "in order to fill the space . . . " or "in order to make a composition" you "divide the panel in two horizontally and then divide it vertically. In the centre you put a large mass, and by lines (always the same, mind) you connect the sides with the central mass." Or you are told to divide any space into small squares, and in these squares find a combination of lines which will repeat, and so on.

Will this develop the artistic intelligence? No, certainly not. In order to develop this you must work from nature with the greatest sincerity, copy flowers or leaves, or whatsoever it be, but with the most scrupulous analysis of their character and forms, for nature only reveals herself to him who studies her with a loving eye. In this way the student will find the essence of the spirit of composition—for there is nothing more harmonious, nothing more symmetrical than a flower, a leaf, and above all the human form—notwithstanding all appearance of irregularity. Here are found all the laws of beauty in composition, and the student who copies them sincerely assimilates these laws with his temperament and personality, and creates for himself an ideal, which later on he applies to his own compositions. It is only by obeying that the artist learns to master nature.

Of course, in a decorative composition there must be an interpretation; that is, there must be something more than an exact copy of nature. The grouping of masses, the arrangement of lines must be conceived according to the place which the composition is to occupy, according to the effect which will harmonise with its surroundings. But these lines cannot be taught; they are the personal gain which our conscientious studies from nature have developed and modified by our temperament (and, mind, everybody understands the spirit of nature in his own individual manner), for one thing is certain: you may set twenty students to copy the same model, and, notwithstanding their perfect sincerity, not one of their studies will resemble the others—unless the teacher has imposed on them his way of seeing it.

There is thus all the stronger reason for developing the individual spirit of observation when it is a question of composition, which is entirely the result of sentiment and character.

It follows that everybody has his own way of seeing, feeling, and reproducing, and this is what the master should above all respect in the pupil, for it is this which makes the artist.

Do not let us forget that routine is the greatest enemy to art. And the teaching of composition in the same fashion to every student leads necessarily to routine, and consequently to the killing of all personality by making the student adopt ways and means which belong to the master.

There is nothing more unfortunate for students than a master who is a genius. The student, lost in admiration of this genius, no longer sees for himself, or belongs to himself; he imitates the master, and there results an exaggeration of his typical characteristics, pushed to caricature without his personal *finesse,* and when we see the works of this imitator, however skilful and clever they may appear, they produce on us the effect of an intelligent parrot and inspire us with a feeling of pity.

It is the duty of a genius to uphold the artistic standard, but he should above all abstain from teaching, for he has neither the requisite time nor the strength for the complete self-abnegation that is required of a teacher, and, I say, he must not have it either.

There is a fundamental difference between one who practises only and one who teaches art. The former may be exclusive, unjust in his opinions; he may, nay, he must, believe that he alone knows true art. That passionate conviction will often be his strength. But imagine the teacher to be imbued with this strength and passion, and you will quickly realise how a young student, domineered over and subjugated, would lose all individuality of character and all the delicacy of his nature; he might perhaps acquire skill, but it would be a copy of the master's skill.

A true teacher must exclude the systematic spirit from his judgment. Far from seeming to keep exclusively to one conception of art only, he must understand all those conceptions which have been produced before and must be able to receive from his pupils all the new modes of expression which can still be brought forth; above all, he must never put his own example forward; he should be absolutely impersonal.

The genius teaches by his work, the professor by word and method. People rarely take into account all the qualities which a true teacher should unite in himself. Yet these are numerous and often of a high order; the consideration and the advantages granted to the man who instructs the young generation are, however, rarely in proportion to his services and merit.

The world is sometimes surprised to see such a small number of good teachers, particularly in the artistic branch. It ought rather to be surprised that men of value have allowed themselves by their aptitude for the vocation to be entrapped into such an ungrateful and badly appreciated career.

If a professor gives himself up entirely to teaching, and sacrifices to it even his desire to produce for himself, he is nearly always looked on as an unsuccessful artist. The esteem accorded to a teacher is measured by his success outside teaching. A young master will be asked if he can draw or model a figure, but never if he can demonstrate to others how to do it. All such wrong and unjust views are calculated to drive the best qualified men out of the profession.[1]

Now to come back to our subject. How many minor Stevenses do we see? How many minor Burne-Joneses? The worst of it is that these good people by their bad imitations make us hate what we liked before ; they almost make us regret that the artist had conceived an original idea, which was the personal result of his artistic intelligence, and that he brought forth this new note, of which all the lesser fry give us such imperfect imitations.

Therefore we must allow the student before and above

---

[1] The salaries also which are offered to young men, after having spent twelve years of their life in studying one branch of art, are more than ridiculous,—less than what a fourth-rate cook would earn, and the members of committees who are not ashamed to offer £120 per annum to a young master lack all respect for art and even self-respect. A great deal might be said on this subject, and I hope some day to have an opportunity of saying it.

everything to be himself. We must never impose on him our way of seeing, so that he may be made to believe, even for a minute, that there is none but our own way of composing. On the contrary, we must show him at every moment the different manners of the old and best masters, and the beauty which exists in each of their different styles. To sum up : we must open up his horizon and enlarge it, so that by means of this enlarged vista he may perceive that "Art is infinite," that it knows no limits, and that the experience of his teacher guides him towards developing his own aspirations and does not impose on him those of his master.

It is a great mistake, and unfortunately one too widely spread, to believe that Sculpture or Painting can be perfected by completely forsaking the ground of simple imitation of nature in order to seek exclusively an ideal type of the objects they represent ; this is to ignore the resources of nature and the results of the infinite multiplicity of accidents which she brings about.

With regard to invention I should like to strike a note of warning : Every and any artist must persuade himself, that frequently what he takes for an invention is only a matter of memory, a souvenir. But however richly stored his memory may be, and however exact, it cannot make up for the constant observation of nature in its infinite variety, for every object in nature and every view of the same object produce entirely new aspects, the study and close observation of which may lead to the discovery of a new beauty,—a discovery which everybody makes according to his light.

There is nothing more conducive to develop the power of composition than work from memory. The student should set himself the daily task of sketching from memory at night what he has done from nature during the day. And if he has seriously set himself this task, he will in his work from nature unconsciously study the characteristic side, the typical side of the action, the large lines, etc. He will no longer be inclined to look at details only, but at the essentials of all those things that go to make the typical.

Further, by combinations of lines which he will be obliged to create, he will see their relation to others and will apprehend their harmony ; in a word, he will develop his personal gift of observation, for the artist is nothing more nor less than an observer, and he is the greater or lesser artist according to the perfection or imperfection of this power of observation.

Begin this memory practice by at first only reproducing the principal lines of what you have done during the day, by reproducing what has appeared most striking to you in the individuality of the model which you had before your eyes, and as your study progresses you will also pass on to the details in your drawing from memory. You should thus reproduce not only your daily studies, but anything which has struck your attention during the day : a typical head, a group of persons in the street, an incident, an accident. And if you make a mental resolve : "To-night I will reproduce this scene," your mind will at once take note of the chief lines of a group, of the division of the masses, down to the movements of each individual and his or her contribution to the elucidation of the subject or incident. Thus unconsciously you will do the work of composition, and you will have done it in your own individual way, for when you sit down at night to reproduce the scene, you will probably only indicate the essential part of the composition as expressed by the large lines, and you will complete it with the details that your own artistic feeling suggests.

In this way, by observing nature, you will get your best teaching, your brain will be stocked with notes which will have become your own property, for they will be assimilated to your temperament and will be a fruitful store to draw upon in the future.

And moreover, having to practise drawing from memory, you will be compelled to observe quickly, and this will help you in the studies from nature to see quickly what is typical in the model or in any subject.

You ought to begin these memory exercises with simple

things, and gradually take up more complicated subjects. You will be surprised at first to find how very little you do remember, but you will rapidly develop your memory power and will note what a resource it may become for an artist. I have practised this work from memory very much, and I well remember how at first I found it impossible to remember anything whatever, but when I closed my eyes and concentrated all my energy and will-power to see again the scene I wanted to reproduce, it would appear to my mental eye in every detail. As soon as I opened my eyes it disappeared, and nothing but white paper lay in front of me; but by repeating the same process several times, I would succeed in fixing the picture on my mental retina, and after having rapidly indicated the principal action of the scene in a few lines, I would close my eyes again to see the details and fill them in. This was my way of proceeding, which I give you for what it is worth. There are probably other ways of arriving at the same result.

In any case it is an excellent practice which makes us study not only the model in the studio in a set pose, but the movements and actions of different beings, all of them contributing to the expression and development of the scene passing before them. And I maintain that it is the best preparation for original composition, for things and scenes we have seen have naturally a greater force than those we invent. It remains our task, in full freedom to idealise, amplify, and to accentuate the scene, and thus to add our personal note to that of nature, and I may go so far as to say, that involuntarily we strike an individual note in everything we reproduce sincerely, as everything which we have seen and which we draw must have passed through our brain, and must thereby have been modified by our own mental point of view.

I do not hold with absolute rules on Composition. Let your compositions be the result of your own mental tendencies, of your feelings and emotion about those things you love best in Nature, and which attract you unconsciously. By these means only can you have the strength of conviction in your work.

It is a difficult question which each one must put to himself some day : What do I love best in Nature ? What characters appeal most to me ? What moves and excites me most ? It seems very simple at first sight, but not so on closer observation. For we see so many works of art, we read so many criticisms — mostly written by very ignorant persons, but written in fine pompous language, in sonorous phraseology which dazzles us,—that we are every minute distracted from our own road, and occasionally it becomes impossible to find ourselves again.

Lucky he who discovers himself, that is, his own bent,

early; he has the chance of becoming a great artist if he is strong enough to resist the direction and advice of others, who, not being able to enter into his identity, would like to see him after their pattern. He who has the strength to avoid this rock, he who has conviction and faith, and along with them an unlimited love for his art, has the gates of fame open to him; he will do good original work, and not develop into an intelligent parrot.

Although composition is an advanced branch of study and of an entirely different order to the work from Nature, you must not think that it is necessary to defer its practice until you have reached an advanced degree of execution; no, rather from the beginning try it, set yourself subjects and try to do them as well as possible, or if not set subjects, try at least things you have seen which have left an impression.

Do such compositions by yourself, but it will be well to show them all some day to your master. In those naïve compositions which are quite your own idea and work, he will see the bent of your mind and the talent which guided you in them; he will derive from them a clue to your temperament, and understand in what direction he will have to guide you, and he will often in the very faults and repetitions find an indication of quality.

I have frequently had such examples before my eyes;

such faults are sometimes only exaggerations of an innate feeling, and if the master perceives that they are often recurring, he ought to strive to detect the personal quality, and he should make the student see and feel gradually that he is exaggerating unduly and that modification will improve without destroying his individuality.

The teacher should prove a physician to his student ; he should auscultate him carefully and frequently ; he should learn to know his temperament and ideas, and prescribe him the needful remedy : two doses of Michel Angelo to this one, three doses of Phidias to that one, and so on ; and he should give the doses in a well gilt and sugared coating, so that the student could never scent the direction which the teacher tries to give to the execution of his ideas : thus he will digest the correction and profit by it.

Would it not be ridiculous if a hospital doctor were one day to order an emetic to all the inmates of his ward without taking into account their varied, perhaps opposite, ailments and wants ? It would be just as absurd if a master were to correct the compositions of all his students in the same fashion, after an invariable method, however different they might be.

The study from the human figure is very different ; it is based on invariable principles of construction, on anatomy, in fact, on positive laws ; and from the beginning these laws

must be taught to all in the same way, because this knowledge ranks almost as a science. But when the student has
well grasped it, loosen the reins and let him show his own
power and accentuate what he has learned.

If a student more or less appropriates the characteristics
of another artist, I should like to tell him of a correction
which years ago my old master dealt me. I had one day,
in very bad taste, introduced a figure group which I had
seen in a bad artist's work. My professor, who easily de-
tected the theft, told me : " In art one must never steal
except from the richest and best. This is very good and
true, but it is still better not to steal at all. We should
instruct ourselves from good works of art, admire without
restriction what appeals most to us in them and draw all the
lessons we can from them, but that does not mean that we
should copy them ; we assimilate their qualities, and they
get transformed in us by our character which, on the other
hand, becomes modified as our study advances, as we progress,
and as we overcome the difficulties."

Beginners are easily satisfied with themselves, particularly
amateurs, who see no further than what is just before them,
who will only study enough to emerge from the state of
knowing nothing, and yet want to go in directly for " ideal "
work. They see in their slightest efforts the realisation of
their dream, and are surprised that others do not see an

equal amount of beauty. I shall not waste words on them beyond saying that they are wanting in respect for art and true artists.

Discouragement, if we are fortunate enough to be discouraged, is always a sign of progress; every time we are discouraged, it means that we have caught fresh glimpses of the beauty of Nature. Let that be a consolation to you and, on the other hand, be wary of satisfaction.

An artist who is satisfied with his work is, artistically speaking, nearing his end, for he will no longer strive to advance and rise; and in Art, when we do not go forward, we go backward. Nature keeps the artist up in the striving after progress, but, unfortunately, when he has attained to a certain celebrity orders crowd in and the temptation is great to scamp the work in order to begin another commission. His work will then rest solely on what he previously learnt, he will repeat himself and sometimes see and feel how inferior his present work is to his earlier productions, but he will not understand that, if he would only go to Nature, she would give him new inspirations; for Nature is as generous as she is beautiful, and does not abandon those who love her. By working from Nature one never runs the risk of absolutely commonplace work.

So let it again be said that the observation of Nature is the fountain whence the artist derives courage, and which gives to his work the character and variety in which she abounds, so that unconsciously, by adding his own interpretation, his work will bear the stamp of individuality.

---

Before speaking of composition in relief, I shall say a few words about the different treatment which is demanded for the different places the relief may have to occupy.

There are three distinct divisions of relief : high-relief, half-relief, and low-relief, and of course a variety of degrees between these. And it is not a matter of indifference which of the varied reliefs should be applied to the decoration of a building.

### High-Relief

The first fact to be realised is, that every projection casts shadows, and that every flat surface attracts and reflects light.

Hence it follows that high-relief is proper for work which will be exposed to full daylight, and which, being placed in the highest part of an architectural monument, can only be seen from a distance.

The Greeks in their best time used relief almost as high as the round for the sculptures adorning the Pediments of their temples (Fig. 99 and Fig. 100), the Metopes in their Doric architecture and the external Friezes. Had these reliefs been less prominent, these wonderful works of sculpture would have been killed by the diffused light, that is, they would have become quite indistinct.

## HALF-RELIEF

In half-relief the objects and figures are only presented in half their natural projection. For works placed outside and at a considerable height, this is not suitable and satisfactory. The figures have not sufficient prominence to give them the appearance of roundness; at least, the spectator is not able to make out at a glance which parts stand out and which retreat. The forms and outlines become indistinct at a distance, because the shades of the figures lose themselves in the cast shadows and their light parts hardly stand out against the light on the wall.

Sculpture in half-relief is therefore suitable for interior decoration, or for easily accessible places. The Ancients made a very happy use of half-relief in applying it to objects of round form, such as vases, the shaft of a column (columnæ celatæ), as in the temple of Diana at Ephesus, or the balustrade of a sacred well. It is easily understood, that in these cases figures modelled in the round would not only destroy the convexity and thus injure the graceful form of the object, but would also render the parts indistinguishable from a distance.

Low-relief, or bas-relief as it is called, to designate its little depth, is particularly adapted to work which is placed in rather dark situations. Its most famous example in antique art is the Frieze of the Parthenon. This was executed in low-relief, because it received no direct light. Being placed within the Colonnade and on the upper part of the wall, it received nothing but reflected light, and could only be seen distinctly when the marble pavement reflected the sunlight on to it.

It stands to reason that a higher and more accentuated relief would have multiplied the shadows in the shade and rendered the work indistinct. In order to make this frieze in its high place more distinct, the outlines are very neatly and sharply cut into the background, forming almost a right angle to the projection, so that the masses of the figures are strongly detached and the flatness of the relief is enhanced by the shadow of its contours, and the eye can easily follow these outlines containing the relieved figures of the composition of the frieze.

In the cases of superposed forms, as, for instance, where an arm crosses the torso, or when the leg of a rider projects on the side of his horse, the part most in projection is quite flat in order that its shadow should not cut up the form

behind it and thus take away from its projection, nor inter-
fere with the more essential shadows which outline the movement of the composition.

Composition in low-relief presents relatively less difficulty
than composition in the round. As it is always executed
on a background, and consequently has only one aspect,
all our efforts are concentrated on the arrangement of this
aspect. On the other hand, in a composition in the round,
whether it be a single figure or a group of several, you have
to consider and express the subject from every aspect, and
to make your lines harmonise and be interesting from every
point of view. Again, as relief approaches painting you can
allow yourself any number of figures in it, all of which will
contribute to explain the subject.

Other difficulties, which I shall enlarge upon as we go
deeper into the subject, compel me to advise you to begin
your design studies in sculpture with compositions in relief,
and not in the round as with the studies from the living
model.

In your first attempts you should limit yourself to a subject
which requires only one or two figures, such as " Music,"
" Poetry," and so on. Later on, when you have acquired
practice in the harmonizing of lines, the effects of shadows,
half-tints and light, you should take mythological subjects
requiring more figures.

When you arrange in relief a subject of one figure, the first question is to find a pose which will best express the idea you wish to represent ; next the contrasts of planes and lines, of which this pose is capable ; then the arrangement of drapery (if the subject admits of drapery) which will best agree with the lines of the figure, and whose folds shall contribute to enhance the action ; and lastly the accessories which will explain the subject to the spectator.

The proportions of these attributes or emblems are highly important; if they are made too big, they risk destroying the scale of the figure, and if too small, they will appear petty ; your taste must guide you in the choice of their proportions.

In a sketch, as well as in the execution in large proportions, every figure that is to be draped afterwards must be modelled in the nude first. Yet at the very first it is necessary to sketch in the complete subject, with figure, drapery, and accessories, so as to have an idea of the general effect. (See Fig. 101.)

When you have made up your mind, that is, when you believe you have conceived the best expression of the subject, the arrangement of lines and places, and fixed the space of every accessory, you should make a sketch of the whole ; afterwards scrape off everything that is in your way, viz. drapery and accessories, and proceed to model the nude of the figure in its large lines, paying special attention to settling the proportions

FIG. 101.—GENERAL EFFECT OF COMPOSITION.

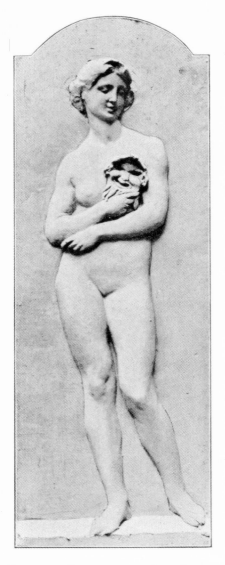

FIG. 102.—COMPOSITION IN LOW RELIEF,
NUDE PREPARATION.

as exactly as possible in the nude (Fig. 102); for it might easily happen in the first hasty sketch that drapery hides the true proportion of an arm, of the leg, or the torso, and when you come to the execution of the design in large size, where the proportions are attended to more carefully, it would be impossible to obtain the same pleasing effect which you accidentally obtained in the sketch.

I know, you cannot always have a living model in front of you, which would at once show you what is possible or impossible in a movement, but what you can and ought to do is—as I have already recommended in my notes on the posing of the living model—to try the pose and movement yourself, to give the expression required for the subject, to observe the place and action of the hands, their relation to the act and the place of the head ; for in the relation of these points you will find the mimic expression of the pose. You should in reality play and act the part represented by the figure you are designing, for you can hardly expect a professional model to evolve out of his or her inner consciousness the feeling and expression which you require, if you have not given him or her an exact rendering of it yourself. It is only on those conditions that you can obtain from the model, if not the exact expression, at least the leading lines, the points of vigour and of rest of the pose.

When you have finished modelling your figure in the

nude, see to the arrangement of the draperies as you had previously indicated them in your small sketch, in its principal lines and masses. I always advise the student before beginning the drapery, to make in clay a replica of his figure in exactly the same pose as the sketch, but in higher projection (Fig. 103)—even in the round, if you like—and to drape it with a piece of muslin or other material. (This will, by the way, be an excellent practice in learning how to manage and arrange drapery on a lay-figure.) Thus you will have a model, which, even if you do not copy it exactly, can suggest to you combinations of lines such as you always find in nature. It remains for you to leave out some folds, or enlarge others, in your sketch; in fact, to utilise whatever can further your design and improve its quality.

If your sketch is of small proportions, it is desirable to damp the drapery which you put on the self-made lay-figure. It will thus better follow the movement of the pose, and take of its own accord a better scale of proportions towards the nude (see Fig. 104); if you put the material on dry, the folds are inclined to become too large, and to hide the chief lines of the figure.

I repeat, that you must take from such an arrangement of drapery only what is absolutely useful to your sketch, for if you copied every detail the result would be confusion and the destruction of the unity of the design. (Fig. 105.)

Fig. 103.—Nude Figure in High Relief for Arrangement of Drapery.

FIG. 104.—DRAPERY ARRANGED ON NUDE FIGURE.

You will do well to repeat the exercise of relief composition with one or two figures several times before you try more complicated subjects.

## Composition in Relief with Several Figures

In an historical composition there are other things to be considered than in an arrangement of one or two allegorical figures, where, apart from the style and character, it is only a question of arrangement of lines and distribution of shadow and light.

When you want to compose the representation of a precise scene, you should first prepare yourself for it by reading about the manners, morals, and customs of the epoch in which it took place; by studying the individual character of each of the persons taking part in it; further, by conjuring up before your mental eye the types of figures and faces which will best depict these persons and their different age. Then there are the costumes which subject and scene demand, and which play such an important part in the movement of the figures, for it is evident that a man clad in a heavy cuirass cannot move as lightly as another covered by a simple chlamis; and lastly, the archæology and architecture of the period—its correctness will at once give an authentic look to the composition. To sum up, you must try to transpose yourself in thought to the period in which the scene passes that you mean to describe. It would be ridiculous to seat a Greek general on a fifteenth century chair, or to drape with the peplos a thirteenth century queen. Yet similar mistakes are often seen in the work of students, who fancy that the only thing needful for a sculptor is to learn how to handle clay.

By getting a subject up in the way I have indicated, the student is compelled to read largely, and if he chooses his subjects from various epochs he will learn to understand and be imbued with the spirit and character of the different periods of history.

Many young art students start on their art career without any previous literary education and culture. The teacher must with all his might induce them to make up for this lack of culture whilst there is time, else it will be fatal to their future artistic creations.

By studying attentively the authors who treat of our subject, we make our study in composition all the more interesting and characteristic, and at the same time, we acquire historical and archæological knowledge.

Having become familiar with the personages in your design, you must begin to play or act their part. You have to ask yourself: in what way, by what change of posture, would this man express such or such a sentiment? It is

FIG. 105.—SKETCH COMPLETED—"COMEDY."

obvious that a person with a cool, deliberate disposition will not gesticulate in the same way as another with an enthusiastic temperament. Sly Ulysses will not reveal his emotions in the manner of impetuous Achilles, nor will Helena act like Iphigenia. The gestures of any of these personages must be different in whatever situation they may be. The difference of natural gesture is consequently well worth studying, for gesture is not only different in individuals, that is, modified by each person's disposition, it varies also in character according to manners and ideas pertaining to different climates, and every nation stamps it with her individual genius. Picture to yourself, for instance, the reserve of an Englishman as opposed to the laughing gesticulation of a Neapolitan. What a difference between the two! And yet notwithstanding all variety, the origin and root of gesture lies in the human heart, in which you may find every shade between the extremes, and by observing the gesticulation of each nation and race the artist will acquire a good scale of gradations. But in reproducing these, his taste will have to decide where to emphasise without becoming vulgar.

You must try then to reveal by the gestures the character of each person—make it, as it were, a biography. Having thus well imagined the scene to be represented and tried to play the part of each actor in turn, begin to group your personages in such a way that they all contribute, according to their importance, to explain the subject. Do not put in any unnecessary figures which would only lead to confusion, but try to get contrasts of age and height, that is, of course, if the subject will allow of it; introduce an old man, an adult, a child, a woman, a young girl, etc., to help towards obtaining variety of form, and thus rendering the design more interesting.

It is sometimes a good plan, and we have striking examples of it in Egyptian and Assyrian reliefs, to have a repetition of movement among the personages of secondary importance; but this should be done with great tact, else the composition would become monotonous. For instance, if the principal *motif* of the subject is in the centre of the composition, and the arm-movements of the secondary figures tend towards that centre, the eyes of the spectator will be guided towards it and his attention will be attracted, so that he will easily see what you mean to express.

You will start the actual blocking-in of your composition with the general grouping of the figures in principal and secondary masses. (See Figs. 106 and 106A.) If the figures should be too far from each other, you may take advantage of drapery to unite them and render the masses more compact, or the same result may be achieved by accessories, arms, furniture, architecture, etc.

In a subject where the attention of the spectator is to

FIG. 106.—OUTLINE SKETCH OF COMPOSITION: "ARTEMIS AND ENDYMION."

FIG. 106A.—ROUGH SKETCH OF COMPOSITION.

Fig. 107.—Nude Preparation.

be concentrated on one point, the figures must not be separated as they may be in a frieze representing a procession : as, for instance, the Panathenaean procession in the Parthenon frieze, which is conceived with the decorative purpose of ornamenting an architectural part. On the other hand, an historical relief is generally conceived as a picture. Although this does not prevent its being applicable to architecture, it is so in a different way, for the subject must be concentrated. A frieze may almost be considered as an animated moulding, a band of enrichment that may go all round the building, whilst an historical composition occupies only one part of it. The moral is : the grouping of the figures must be compact.

After having blocked-in the composition in general, you proceed in the same manner as with a single-figure design, that is, you sketch in the nude of all the figures in their large lines and proportions, etc. (see Fig. 107), and if there are draperies you make again lay-figures in clay ; but instead of making them as separate figures, I should advise you to model the figures of the whole composition on a somewhat larger scale than your sketch, and above all in much higher projection (Fig. 108), and then to drape all these figures (see Fig. 109). This will enable you to obtain more harmony of lines in the draperies than if you had arranged each figure separately.

From this drapery arrangement you take, of course, only what is needed for your design, and suppress all the details which might cause confusion and hamper the unity of the design. And *unity* is the true secret of the success of any work. Perhaps you will ask what unity means in a composition? It means a certain general concurrence in the character and choice of the important lines, and the existence of a dominant part in the arrangement to which all the other parts tend.

You must pay great attention to the value of the masses, and avoid having several of the same volume. These latter may pass in a purely decorative allegory, or be even occasionally necessary there to preserve the equilibrium and balance of the architectural feature of which it forms part. But an historical relief applied to an architectural structure is always framed by a moulding, so that the design is already separated from the building by the frame and becomes a sculptural picture, and we may therefore contrast the masses as much as good taste will allow.

Sometimes you will get into difficulties by your masses looking too round or too pyramidal in their contours, and giving to the general design a want of strength and stability. I advise you then to try a few straight lines, either vertical or horizontal, which you may bring in under the plea of an architectural feature. These will assist you

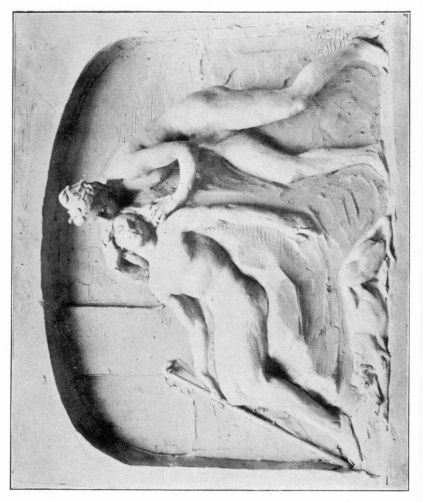

FIG. 108.—NUDE FIGURES IN HIGH RELIEF FOR ARRANGEMENT OF DRAPERY.

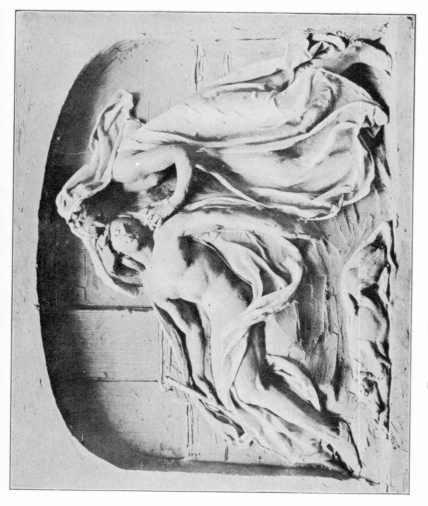

FIG. 109.—DRAPERY ARRANGED ON NUDE FIGURES.

materially in rectifying the balance and unity of the whole. You will observe in Fig. 110, where two masses or groups form an unpleasant angle, a horizontal line unites them and gives simple strength to the composition.

If, on the other hand, the masses in your design are filled with violent gestures in horizontal directions, a vertical

FIG. 110.—SHOWING THE EFFECT OF TWO MASSES HAVING A VERTICAL TENDENCY.

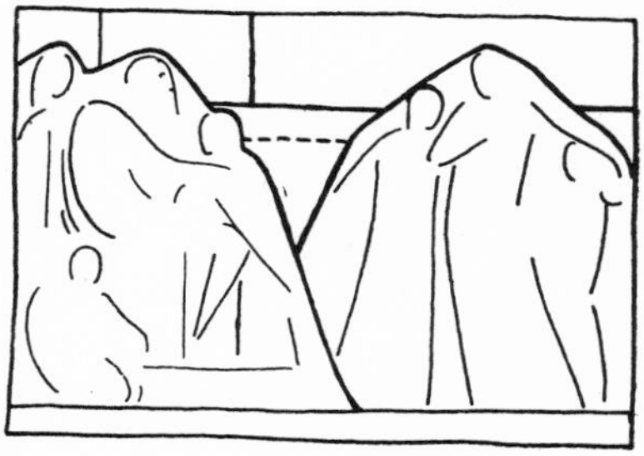

FIG. 110A.—TWO MASSES HAVING A VERTICAL TENDENCY CORRECTED BY HORIZONTAL LINES.

line introduced will not only restore the balance, but also, by contrasting with the accentuated movement of the persons, will heighten the contrast and give more forcible expression to the action (see Fig. 111). The dominant lines which enclose the scene and the movement of each personage may be interrupted by parts which disappear more or less on the background according to the distance or plane on which the figure is to be ; but they should never vanish altogether, or the masses will get weakened and confused, so that the result would be a lack of unity and clearness, for in a relief, seen from a certain distance, what strikes us first is the silhouette of its contours, and these ought to give by their drawing a general idea of the movement and sentiment enacted within their frame.

FIG. 111.—SHOWING THE EFFECT OF TWO MASSES HAVING A HORIZONTAL TENDENCY.

FIG. 111A.—TWO MASSES HAVING A HORIZONTAL TENDENCY CORRECTED BY VERTICAL LINES.

If you wish to shift the mass forward or push it back, or make it more or less projecting, you may with advantage use the following means :—Slice it off by means of a thread, take it carefully off the background, and then lay it on to the right or left of its original place until you have found the most suitable spot, when you fix it by pressing it lightly down in the centre and blending the clay in its outline with the background.

COMPLETED SKETCH: "ARTEMIS AND ENDYMION."

Should you wish to have it in higher relief after having cut it off and removed it, lay some clay on the background in its place until you have the desired projection, and then stick your mass of figures on to this added clay.

If you desire to diminish the projection, proceed in the opposite fashion, that is, after having cut off the mass, scrape some clay off the background and then stick your group on again. By this means you avoid having to remodel entirely what you had already done, and you can judge more quickly of the advantage of the change.

---

I must now deal with a question which has given rise to endless discussions, namely, the introduction of perspective in low-relief sculpture.

The Greek sculptors have always looked at the background of their reliefs as at a solid plane and not as representing air or sky, and everything justifies their point of view. To begin with, the shadows which a relief casts on the surface from which it rises proclaim very clearly the solidity of this surface, whether it be a wall, a vase, or the shaft of a column, for if the marble background should stand for the sky, it would be absurd to let shadows be projected on to it. Secondly, if the sculptor wishes to represent the appearance of a painting, he must progressively diminish the size of the figures which he means to be in the background ; but he will be contradicted by the light, which will strike these figures as strongly as those in the foreground.

It was, therefore, not ignorance which made the Athenians avoid optical effects in sculpture, but rather perfected taste which forbade them to break the gravity of architecture by imitations of paintings which would seem to pierce the wall, and which would be still more unbecoming on a vase or on a column.

Is there in effect anything more offensive to an educated eye and mind than to simulate a concavity on the surface of a convex object, and to alter by an appearance of perspective the integrity of a column or a beautiful vase ?

Surely nobody will imagine that the simple laws of perspective were unknown to the architect Apollodorus, of Damascus, who erected the Column of Trajan ? And yet this lofty column, the spiral of which carried up to the clouds the colossal statue of Trajan and the representation in relief of his battles and sieges in the Dacian war, shows in the background of the relief buildings which do not retreat according to the strict laws of geometrical perspective. The artist has preferred a skilful mistake which respected the roundness of the monument to an awkward observation of graduated planes and vanishing lines, which, hollowed

FIG. 112.—PORTION OF THE RELIEF ROUND TRAJAN'S COLUMN, ROME.

Fig. 113.—Portion of the Frieze of the Parthenon.

FIG. 114.—EASTERN GATE OF THE BAPTISTERY, FLORENCE, BY LORENZO GHIBERTI.

FIG. 115.—RAPE OF THE SABINES, BY GIOVANNI DA BOLOGNA.

out into the drum of the column, would have produced the illusion of a piercing where it was necessary to sustain the idea of indestructible solidity (see Fig. 112).

Phidias avoided the effects of perspective in the frieze of the Parthenon, but was not afraid of introducing in some places an apparent confusion, as, for instance, where he projected equestrian figures on other similar ones. But the repetition of limbs and the superposition of horses turn out to be excellently calculated by the greatest of masters for imitating the embroiled movement of cavalry in motion, and contrasting it with the isolation of the other figures and the quiet dignity of their solemn march (see Fig. 113).

Modern low relief, alas! is very far from Greek art. It has been subjected to the influence of painting, and to realise this you need only compare a specimen of the frieze by Phidias with the doors of the baptistery of St. John at Florence by Lorenzo Ghiberti (see Fig. 114, and Fig. 115 by G. Bologna). Ghiberti has brought in aërial and lineal perspective for the treatment of distance; he represents mountains, trees, sky and clouds, and fancies thereby to have achieved a great progress over antique simplicity. But the brazen solidity of the background belies too clearly the vanishing lines and the illusory distance.

Unfortunately, the Italian and French sculptors of the following century went on in this style of ultra-picturesque sculpture. They wasted all their energy and enthusiasm in piling figure on figure, plane on plane, cutting the marble away from full relief to the lowest half-tone in the background.

You will understand how this childish striving after an impossible illusion injured the purity of form and grandeur of style, how the essential qualities of art were forgotten in carving out unequal dark spots in order to provide the needed half-tones ; in short, how effect was put in the place of beauty. See Fig. 116, Alexander and Diogenes.

I do not mean to imply that all colours should be interdicted in low-relief sculpture, but I want you to understand that it is the significance of the subject which prescribes the general effect of colour in the relief.

Let me conclude by impressing on you that for the principles of modelling in relief you cannot have a better guide and adviser than the models of Greek art, whether you find them in the ornamentation of vases, in tombs or altars, whether they give life to a frieze or to the pediment of a building, or whether they inscribe on the base of a statue those episodes and familiar scenes which go towards explaining the history of the period.

FIG. 116.—ALEXANDER AND DIOGENES, BY PUGET.

## Composition in the Round

In figure composition we must as carefully as in relief composition strive to render the subject well, the harmony of lines, the contrast of planes, &c. ; and in addition to this—and that is the greatest difficulty—we must take care to make our subject clear from every side of the composition. It happens frequently that one or two views are interesting and the others insignificant, and then, in order to invest these latter sides with interest, one is obliged to change the arrangement entirely. On this account composition in the round is a much more complicated work than composition in relief, where all efforts are concentrated on one point of view only. On the other hand, the definite execution of a relief as a study from nature is in its turn more difficult than the execution in the round, in which there is less interpretation, because it comes so near to nature, that it is almost absolute.

When the work in the round consists of a single figure, the difficulty of composition is lessened because one can easily see and understand its action from all sides, but as soon as there are two or three figures, the difficulty begins—perhaps one of the figures may be completely hidden from one point of view, or there may be parts which have the appearance of relief, and yet it is essential that every figure should preserve its roundness, its proportions, and, above all, be interesting from every side.

When for a single figure you have fixed on the action which expresses your subject best, the living model can give you—apart from style—all the qualities you wish to add, and if you have the good fortune to find a suitable model, with the characteristics that your subject requires, you have nothing more to do than to copy it faithfully, amplifying here, accentuating there, its character and type.

Simple poses are always preferable for a single-figure subject, and what is more, are more proper to sculpture, for the first condition of a statue is that it should stand well, should have a solid and firm position, and be so well balanced that the looker-on shall not be alarmed about its equilibrium and durability. It therefore behoves the sculptor to choose a simple action without complications, and to prefer an enduring action to an exceptional fleeting act.

It is painful to look at a statue which wriggles and writhes in violent efforts ; such a statue may impress you for a moment, but if you have it longer before your eyes its contortions tire and trouble you, and you feel inclined to say : " Please, take a little rest."

It is also very annoying to see a head which is laughing outright—it looks so very insipid.

A single figure ought to give us the sensation of stability,

Fig. 117.—Fighting Gladiator.

FIG. 118.—VENUS DE MILO.

and in this respect it comes near to an architectural work, for which one also requires apparent as well as real solidity. The pose of a single figure ought to be such that it can at least be kept without fatigue for a little while.

In a relief or in a painting, when you see one gladiator throwing himself upon another to vanquish him, you feel that his violent action is justified by the presence of the other personage towards whom he hurries. On the other hand, to see a figure in the round rush violently into space without an apparent object is simply ridiculous.

You will understand from this that the sculpture in the round, especially if it is a single figure, is less suited than relief or painting to represent a lively movement; the very material which we employ forbids us to think of representing the illusion of a violent movement as immovable.

The antique statue of the Fighting Gladiator (Fig. 117), an admirable, much admired work, shows deep knowledge of anatomy, and may serve as model in the art of expressing with energy and vivacity the play of the muscles, and elasticity of limbs trembling with life ; its forms are wonderful in drawing and expression—and yet, notwithstanding all these qualities, it is incomplete and fatiguing. If we compare this splendidly executed work with the Venus of Milo (Fig. 118), or, better still, with the group of the Three Fates by Phidias, you understand at once the difference which exists in the quiet grandeur, nobility, and dignity of the latter works and the annoyance or impatience which we feel before the former—notwithstanding our admiration for its technical excellence.

Michel Angelo, who was fond of highly accentuated poses, well understood how to imply a feeling of rest in his sculptural works. If you look at the figures on the Medici tomb (Fig. 119) you cannot fail to admire their stability, notwithstanding their highly accentuated attitudes.

There exist many life-size dancing figures, where the whole weight of the body rests on the point of one toe, and although many of them are perfect in execution, yet they cause a feeling of uneasiness, and are all the more fatiguing to look at, as they are of large proportions. Such subjects for single figures are only excusable on a small scale, and not in marble either, but in bronze.

## EXECUTION OF A SINGLE-FIGURE SKETCH

To make a sketch in the round for a single figure, you can make an armature or skeleton frame-work after the pattern which I have already described for the study from Nature ; the support should be of iron, the rest of lead-piping fastened with copper-wire, and everything in correct proportion to the size of the sketch you are going to make. These sketches

FIG. 119.—FIGURE FROM THE TOMB OF GIULIANO DEI MEDICI, SACRISTY OF ST. LORENZO, FLORENCE.

can be made in clay, modelling paste, or wax. The advantage
in using the two latter materials consists in their not being
liable to drying, which is with
difficulty avoided when you use
clay in a work of small dimensions. In a figure of only ten
inches in height you can re-
place lead-piping by two or
three threads of twisted copper-
wire (Fig. 120); they will occupy less space than the limbs,
and are of a sufficient resistance
to support the material; and
they are also very malleable
or easy to bend. The frame
must be twisted and bent into
the desired action (see Fig. 121),
and then be slightly covered
with whatever material you have
selected to work in, the same as
in a life study, and the correct
proportions should from the beginning be adhered to, otherwise

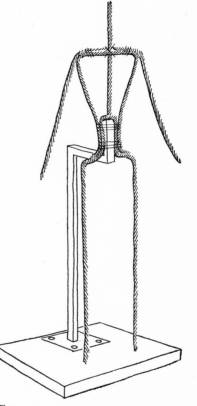

FIG. 120.—ARMATURE IN TWISTED
COPPER WIRE.

it will be difficult to ascertain if the movement is possible;
at this stage it will be easy to turn and twist the figure

until the pose is quite as you wish it to be.   (See Figs. 122
and 123.)

You might twist and turn an informal mass of clay or

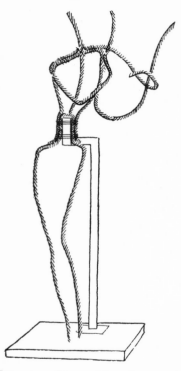

wax in all directions, it would
never convey to you the spirit
of the fineness of the action,
therefore the greatest neatness
is desirable, and is encouraging
at the same time, as it will
help considerably to draw and
reveal the idea which underlies
your composition.

I always advise my students
to try the contrary of what I
say, so that they may become
convinced by their own experience.   It is even desirable to
let students, who doubt the
master's directions, proceed in
their own fashion, so that, if it
is contrary to practical rule,
they should find themselves,

Fig. 121.—Copper Wire (twisted)
Armature in Action.

figuratively speaking, in a morass.   After having allowed
them to flounder and struggle hopelessly for some time, lead
them back into the right way.   That will convince them, and

Fig. 122.—Armature Covered with Clay.

FIG. 123.—COMPLETE SKETCH OF SINGLE FIGURE. THE FIRST SOUND
OF THE LYRE.

give them confidence and faith in the advice of their teacher, which is necessary for their progress.

And here I may as well put in a word for neatness and cleanliness in the modeller's work. It does sometimes appear to me as if students believed that a sculptor ought to look dirty and be covered with clay, and not only have the clay on his garments, but also lying about his modelling-table and on the floor, have his tools and sponge muddy, the linen rags (used to keep his work damp) lying dirty on the floor, with puddles of water about—in fact, the studio to look as disgustingly dirty as certain famous stables of antiquity, which Heracles was set to clean ; and I must reluctantly say that lady-students are the greatest offenders in this direction. Now this proves to me a want of respect for your work, and a want of care and carefulness which is inexcusable. It shows that the student does not take sufficient interest in his study, else he would not surround himself with dirty disorder, which must distract his thoughts from his work.

It is on the other hand necessary to surround yourself and your work with cleanliness and tidiness, to put out of sight everything unnecessary which might unconsciously attract your eye, and to make your work as attractive as possible, so as to enable you to see its faults distinctly and to spend all your care and attention on correcting them.

However childish these details may appear to you, they

are of enormous importance, as I dare say you will find out for yourself by comparing the work of a tidy, methodical student with that of another lacking these qualities.

When you have obtained the action of your figure-sketch to your satisfaction, and the correct proportions, you must try to invest its forms with the character of the person you are to represent, for it is clear that the forms of Heracles will not be suitable for Apollo or Hermes. After that you have to think of the head and the arrangement of the hair —a subject which plays a great part in the style of a statue ; there is nothing which will change the character of a head more than the arrangement of the hair ; if it is done in bad taste, it will invest the whole statue—however good it may in other respects be—with vulgarity. On the other hand, you may often see a nude statue of rather ordinary execution, but where the hair and all the details introduced about it have been done with such taste and care, that the otherwise commonplace statue seems to have style and distinction. The plinth is also of great importance ; its size should never be more than necessary for the statue to rest on, the smaller the plinth, the taller and more elegant the statue will appear ; but if it is unnecessarily large it will detract from the appearance of the statue, just as any other details on too big a scale would do.

If a statue is to be draped, you can employ the same

means as for the relief study, *i.e.*, make on another armature a copy of the nude sketch of the same size, or even somewhat larger, and then drape it with damp drapery. It is more difficult to obtain a satisfactory arrangement of drapery for a statue than for a relief, because it has to look well all round, and the folds on one side must be as carefully attended to as those on the other side; the chief lines of the folds from the front, profile, and back have to be joined, the principal masses have to be settled from every view, and lastly the details.

If you proceed thus carefully in arranging the drapery, there will be harmony and intelligence in the folds, because one set of folds will spring from the other. But if you do not trouble about the whole to begin with, and, having found a pleasing arrangement for the front view, if you copy that by itself and then proceed to make another arrangement for the back and sides, your drapery will lack that feeling of continuity which makes for harmony; there will only be different sets of more or less pleasing folds, which cannot have the clearness of expression that you obtain by the other methods.

Another thing you have to avoid in making a statue is, stretching out the limbs in equal movements, so that they make angles of the same degree, especially right angles; such geometrical figures round the body cannot lend elegance to the composition, for they make the outline hard and take away from its harmony and homogeneity. (See Fig. 124.)

In a kneeling figure you must take care that it should not from one point of view look like a cripple without legs, see Fig. 125. You have rather to contrive the lines of your pose in such a way that the spectator sees sufficient of the legs from every side to prevent such an idea rising in his mind.

If your figure should be posed sitting or climbing on a rock,

FIG. 124.—DIAGRAM SHOWING ANGULAR POSE OF THE LIMBS.

you must not give too much importance to the rock by making it too big, see Fig. 126, else your figure would look like a toy on the rock and lose its sculptural aspect ; you must rather reduce the rock to the minimum of what is necessary to give the figure a solid footing or seat. In short, everything about a statue in the

FIG. 125.—DIAGRAM OF A KNEELING FIGURE, GIVING THE APPEARANCE OF A CRIPPLE.

round which is not the figure itself should be considered as a detail and not to be made much of, but should nevertheless be executed in good taste.

The action for a single figure as well as for a group in sculpture is suggested to the artist, or perhaps I should say limited, by the purely material necessities of his art ; he has to vary them with the different materials employed in sculpture.

Before I start on the subject of composition of groups, I must say a few words on these different materials and on the action and gesture they permit.

There are four materials principally employed in sculpture : Wood, Marble, Bronze, and Terracotta.

Fig. 126.—Diagram showing an Exaggerated Proportion of the Rock to the Figure.

## Wood

Sculpture in wood is more suitable for gesture than in stone and marble. A fibrous, compact, and comparatively light substance, wood has more power of bearing than stone and marble, and consequently it can be projected further. The limbs of a figure carved in oak, cedar, or walnut, when stretched out from the body, do not run the risk of breaking with their own weight. A lively and expanded gesture, which would be impossible in marble, is quite possible and tolerable in wood-carving, where it will cause no uneasy feeling to mind and eye.

Although wood-carving has been and is still applied to large figures, it is really more suitable for work of smaller dimensions which can be carved out of one piece. In any case it is for interior decoration, sheltered from the inclemency of the weather, that one should employ a material which is liable to split. Besides being liable to the risk of being consumed by fire and eaten by worms, wood cannot promise the artist a long duration, that is, a duration in proportion to the time, patience, and skill spent on and required by the material, for the practice of wood-carving is not learnt as quickly as that of marble-carving, it requires much greater skill in the handling of tools.

## MARBLE

Of all the materials employed in sculpture, marble is the least suitable for violent action, and the simple, almost solemn, attitudes which the Greek sculptors gave to their statues were advised by the weight of the material.

For this very reason marble is very well suited for sculpture, as it compels the artist to observe a tranquillity of line and severity of outline favourable to the grand style, by rendering bold action and violent gesture impossible.

Thus it is needful for a sculptor to be quiet and grave when he works for marble, but this restraint imposed on his genius will turn out an advantage.

Sculpture in marble, on account of its robust and masculine simplicity, might be called the Doric order of Statuary. Its movement should be concentric, not eccentric.

## BRONZE

Before speaking of what is permissible in bronze, I will try to give you a summary sketch of bronze-casting, which may make it easier for you to understand its possibilities as a medium for the expression of your ideas.

The art of bronze-casting, which goes back to very ancient times, as bronze was known before iron, was brought to high perfection by the Greeks.

Within recent years the method of casting bronze in sand-moulds, which had been used for a century, has largely given way to the older so-called " à cire perdue " process, where the wax model is melted out of the complete mould, and which is now even applied to colossal statues.

The sculptor who wishes to have his clay model repro-

duced in bronze must first cast it in plaster of Paris. From
the plaster statue a new mould must be taken, either a
piece-mould in plaster of Paris or a gelatine-mould. The
latter process saves to a large extent the retouching on
the wax cast, as there is but one seam instead of the
numerous seams of a piece-mould. The new mould is then,
by means of a brush, covered with layers of a liquid wax
composition until the desired thickness has been obtained,
for you must bear in mind that the place of the wax will
afterwards be taken by the bronze. When the pieces of
the mould covered with wax have been joined, they are
tied round with iron strips, and through an opening left at
the bottom a liquid mixture, consisting of powdered brick
and plaster, is poured into the mould to fill it completely
and form the core for the bronze. In larger work it is
necessary to have an iron armature inside the core to give
support to the bronze. This core will adhere closely to the
wax when hardened, so that when the iron bands, the plaster-
shell, and the gelatine-mould are taken off, the statue supported by the core stands before you in wax. This is the
moment when the sculptor has to repair any damage wrought
in places during the casting process, especially where the
mould has left seams at the joints.

When the wax model has been touched up, it becomes
necessary to insert small rods of bronze through the wax

into the core, and to let them stand out in order to join the outer mould to the core and to sustain the latter in place when the wax form has been melted. The bronze-caster also puts in a few ducts for the outflow of the wax which does not get absorbed by the mould and core, and in various places vents or ducts for the escape of air during the casting process, and lastly the "ingates" through which the liquid metal is to flow into the mould. Then the figure is covered by a carefully prepared liquid mixture of clay, pounded brick, and plaster, laid on in several layers so as to form a strong outer shell. It is a process that takes time and cannot be hurried, as any air-bubbles or any hidden place left uncovered will prove damaging to the work. When thoroughly dry the whole is placed in the casting-pit, and through the application of continuous heat the wax is melted and driven out through the prepared canals, but part of it gets absorbed by the mould and core, and helps to strengthen them. I believe the bronze-caster can calculate the proportion that ought to flow out, and thus be quite sure that every particle of wax has left the space which is to be filled with bronze.

When everything has been prepared and the precautions that practice suggests have been taken, the liquid metal is poured into the mould, and, if no accidents happen, it will rise gradually and fill every space of the mould.

How exciting and what anxious work the casting itself is has been most dramatically described by Benvenuto Cellini when he cast his statue of Perseus.

When the metal has been cooled the outer shell is carefully broken off, the core is raked out, and the pieces of metal representing the ducts and any other unevennesses are removed. Then the sculptor sees his work transformed into an enduring material before him.

Do not imagine that this superficial description is meant to instruct you in bronze-casting or to invite you to try it yourself. My only object in sketching the process is to explain to you how the laws governing movement in sculpture are modified by the nature of the material. A bronze statue is, indeed, comparatively light, although modern bronze-casters do not economise the material in the same degree as the ancients did, and this possibility of lightness permits the artist to have figures with outstretched limbs and flowing draperies which could not be done in marble. It permits him to lighten the weight in these overhanging parts by having a thinner coat of wax in their place in the mould, and, again, to increase the weight at the bottom to better support the superstructure. Bold poses and actions may be attempted in bronze without exciting anxiety so long as the laws of gravity and the dignity of art are respected.

## TERRACOTTA

The word means fired clay, but it is also applied to the unburnt clay. The use of burnt clay has not been restricted to the potters of antiquity, but was well known to the sculptor in very ancient times, and works which have been found in Egyptian tombs of the earliest times in Etruscan and Greek excavations prove that this branch of art is as old as that of the potter.

In the middle ages terracotta was not much used; large statues that were not executed in stone or metal were formed in stucco and painted, but from the fifteenth century downwards great artists have not disdained to leave us their work in terracotta. I only mention here the beautiful portrait busts of which you find examples in the South Kensington Museum and the enamelled terracottas of the della Robbias. Though the art declined in the seventeenth and eighteenth centuries, the latter half of the nineteenth century saw a revival of it, and it is much to be hoped that terracotta will gradually take the place of the much less durable plaster in architectural decoration.

Terracotta statues are generally produced in the following manner. The clay model is cast in plaster in the same way as for reproduction in marble or bronze, and on this plaster-cast a piece-mould is made, consisting of numerous pieces which can be drawn out of the deep and under-cut parts of the model without damaging it or each other, and which are one and a half to two inches thick. At the back of each piece a mark is made by gouging out a hole about half an inch deep, and when the front of the statue has been covered with pieces, they are brushed over with soap or clay-water and covered by a uniform layer of plaster about two inches thick strengthened with pieces of iron. Having thus moulded the front part, you go on to the moulding of the back of your statue, and proceed in the same way, only instead of enclosing the back pieces in one large shell of plaster you make four or five of them. Then take the outer shell off the front, and draw all the small pieces off the statue, beginning with the last piece, and putting them carefully in their places in the shell, which you will easily find owing to the gouged-out holes, which represent raised points in the shell. You do the same with the other pieces at the back, and put each small piece in place in the outer shell. This constitutes a piece-mould.

The mould is then dusted over with French chalk to prevent the clay from adhering, and then carefully prepared clay, rather harder than it is used for modelling purposes, is pressed or squeezed into the piece-mould, beginning with the front of the statue. Care is taken to make this layer of clay of an even thickness, so that in drying the shrinkage shall be everywhere the same and no cracks occur.

The front half being finished you go on to the back, and begin with the part containing the head ; when that is finished you join it at once to the front, and put your hand inside to press the clay of the front and back pieces carefully together so that they form one mass. In the same way the succeeding pieces are treated, and when all the parts are joined, strong cords are put round the outer shell, and the clay is left to settle and get firm in the mould for a day or longer. After that the mould, which was hitherto in a horizontal position, is raised to the vertical, the cords undone, the outer shell of the front is taken off, and the pieces of the mould are carefully drawn off and at once replaced in the shell for further use. The back is treated in the same way, but a few pieces at the base are left as support, in case the clay should not be firm enough to support the weight of the upper portion. Where the mould has been taken off the work must be retouched, the seams must be taken off, and a touch here and there will give freshness to the work. Of course this ought to be done at once before the clay gets too hard, for it is not advisable to damp the surface again, as the moisture would run down and impair its solidity at the base. The work of taking a piece-mould from a relief is the same, but much simpler, as one shell is sufficient to enclose all the pieces.

A good number of proofs may be taken out of the same piece-mould, and the proofs are put carefully away for months to dry before they are committed to the kiln for firing. Through the action of firing they become as hard as marble, and better fitted than marble to withstand the damaging influence of our treacherous climate.

The shrinkage during drying and firing is about one in thirteen, which explains to you why work intended for firing cannot be supported by an iron or wooden framework inside ; the latter would remain rigidly the same, and would cause the clay to crack and break when it shrinks.

Apart from this process, sculptors occasionally venture to have small sketches fired without having recourse to the above rather expensive process. There is a charm in the idea of preserving an original clay–sketch, inspired and worked with feverish haste, being quite spontaneous in design and execution. But even such sketches must submit to the laws of gravity and the fragility of the material. You will occasionally find it advisable to cut off an outstretched arm or a flowing drapery, to mould and squeeze it separately, and fix it after firing by means of plaster and inserted wires.

I have given you only a very general description of the process of making terracotta reproductions, in order to enable you to understand what is permissible in the material. There are a great number of details which no description of mine could teach you, and into which only practice under a skilled moulder and caster can initiate you.

## Composition of Groups

A group in the terms of sculpture means an assemblage of figures united by a common motive or a common action, and so close together that the eye can take them in all at once, and thus perceive the effect which the artist has intended.

It is action which gives life to Art; its object is the representation of the human passions and the action of the human will, so as to appeal to the eye and the emotion of the spectator.

But the passions and actions of men do not usually reveal themselves in remote solitude. A forced action in a single figure borders on madness, and is as rare as its representation in sculpture would be insipid.

Laocōon as a single figure dying in the terrible coils of the snake would not call forth our pity to the same extent as the group where his young children are joined with their father in the death-struggle with the monsters.

In the conception of a group the sculptor takes a step

which brings him nearer to low-relief. In whatever material the group is to be executed, the artist is allowed to depict more movement than in a single figure ; not only because, by the arrangement of the figures he can find combinations of lines and poses which may serve as points of support to the figure whose action is more developed, but also because a violent action will be justified by the presence of another figure of the group.

A group of two, if both figures are to be standing, is certainly one of the most difficult tasks in sculpture. If the subject, to be clearly understood, demands that both personages shall face the spectator, the back view of the group cannot be very interesting, being without the two principal factors of expression, the faces ; there will only be two backs to be seen, and the front must necessarily show the only interesting view. This is only one of the rocks to be avoided, but there are a good many others, for the law which rules the single-figure composition, namely, that it should be interesting from every side, obtains also for the group of two or more figures, and therefore it is obvious that you must avoid evident repetition of forms and lines.

A difference between the two figures in sex, age, or height is a great help towards this, and the contrast between the nude and drapery may also help to break the monotony ; the placing of the figures at different heights at the base

will supply another *motif* of outline and happier grouping,
than if both figures were placed on the same level. If the
subject permits it, an accentuated movement will contrast with
a quieter, more dignified one ; in short, more than anywhere

Fig. 127.—Diagram showing Apparent Cutting Off
of the Back Figure.

else, this is the occasion where contrast must be used to
avoid the monotony to which a group of two is liable.

The difficulty will be lessened if one of the figures is
seated or reclining, and then again, it may not be possible
to see from the front view the legs of the figure that is
behind the reclining one (see Fig. 127), and from the back the
sitting figure may not be visible. In short, there are endless

difficulties, and I have just mentioned a few because "fore-warned is forearmed."

There is plenty of scope here for your individual taste to try and find combinations which will avoid these pitfalls. My own opinion about groups of two figures is that they should be placed in front of a wall, in fact, that they should form part of its decoration, so that all the sculptor's energy could be spent on the front view, and that it might be composed as a high-relief.

It is easier to give to the composition an aspect of roundness when you have to make a group of three figures in which there are differences of age or height. If they are placed at different heights on the plinth the composition of lines is less constrained, and there is less risk of repetition in the views. Still, here also you must avoid concentrating in one point of view what will explain the subject : the latter must be comprehensible from all sides.

When the general conception of a group of several figures is ready in your brain and imagination, make a first small sketch from about six to eight inches high. Throw a lump of clay on your stand, and knock it into the general shape that you have conceived, without first troubling much about the movement of each figure (as a composer would hum the melody and not trouble about the orchestration in his first sketch). Look out rather for the planes of contrast of

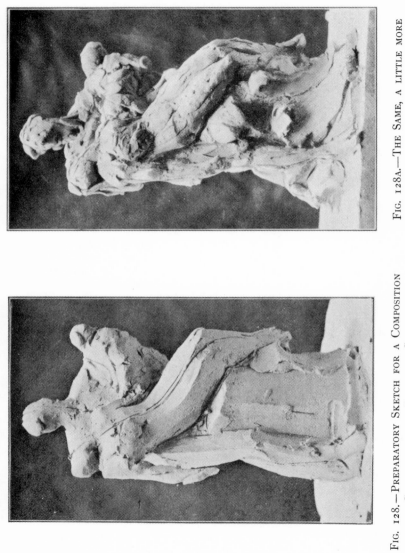

FIG. 128.—PREPARATORY SKETCH FOR A COMPOSITION CARVED OUT OF A BLOCK OF CLAY.

FIG. 128A.—THE SAME, A LITTLE MORE ADVANCED.

which your first plan is capable; then mark with small balls of clay the position of the heads of the various figures to indicate the places whence the movement may develop. Draw this by its chief lines in the planes which you have discovered first, then the arms and legs will find their place. (See Figs. 128 and 128A.)

By thus evolving your composition out of a lump of clay the group becomes more compact, it has a sculptural quality which it would not have if the figures were modelled separately and then grouped. The latter proceeding does not give brilliant results, and I have seen groups of three figures, where the six legs looked like six posts supporting three unhappy torsos. You will at least avoid that by starting your sketch with a solid mass of clay and avoiding unnecessary perforations. Michel Angelo has laid down the rule that a group should be so compactly composed that, if it is rolled down a hill, none of the limbs would break off, and he was certainly right in principle, although the formula sounds daring.

When the indication of planes and their combinations suggests the movement, you must examine how far this agrees with the feeling that each of the personages is to express. It is here even more necessary than in a relief that unity should prevail, not only in the *ensemble* of the composition, but also in the expression and gesture of the figures. The famous actor Garrick, in commenting on the acting of a friend, who played the part of a drunken man, reproved him by saying that his head was completely drunk, but that his arms and legs were quite capable—thus insisting on unity in gesture. In fact, an enraged man, who is ready to fight, will not simply express his fury in his face : his whole body will show the preparation for the fight, his tendons will be strained for attack or resistance, his muscles will quiver with excitement, his attitude will correspond with the emotion that possesses him. A despairing man, on the other hand, who has lost courage, will appear as if all vital force had left him, his pose, his limbs will seem uncontrolled, his muscles slack, in short, everything will express his state of mind. So you must observe it is not the head alone which expresses this or that feeling, but the whole figure.

You should always be thoroughly imbued with the feeling you want to express and to excite in the spectator, and I repeat what I have insisted on before, you should try conscientiously to act the part of the man you want to represent, to make yourself well acquainted with him by reading, and to try to realise with your mental eye the scenes you read of in poetry.

When you are satisfied with the general effect of your small sketch, with its outline, its movement, and planes, it will be necessary to begin a second sketch in larger proportions,

FIG. 129.—EXAMPLE OF A COMPOSITION IN THE ROUND FOR A GARDEN.

EXAMPLE OF A COMPOSITION IN THE ROUND FOR A GARDEN.

EXAMPLE OF A COMPOSITION IN THE ROUND FOR A GARDEN.

in which you will in a more definite way fix the movement of each personage, trying at the same time to preserve the compact mass of the first sketch. When the movement is settled, the exact proportioning of the limbs will follow, and then you will proceed to the execution of the work in the way I have already described for composition in general.

I hope that these instructions will help you to overcome some of the innumerable difficulties which our Art presents to the beginner.

I intend to complete the series by another volume in which I shall treat of the modelling of animals, and of the different methods of enlargement of statues from small sketches, and of different armatures for colossal work, for equestrian statues, etc.

FINIS.

Dover Books on Art

# Dover Books on Art

*ART ANATOMY, Dr. William Rimmer.* One of the few books on art anatomy that are themselves works of art, this is a faithful reproduction (rearranged for handy use) of the extremely rare masterpiece of the famous 19th century anatomist, sculptor, and art teacher. Beautiful, clear line drawings show every part of the body—bony structure, muscles, features, etc. Unusual are the sections on falling bodies, foreshortenings, muscles in tension, grotesque personalities, and Rimmer's remarkable interpretation of emotions and personalities as expressed by facial features. It will supplement every other book on art anatomy you are likely to have. Reproduced clearer than the lithographic original (which sells for $500 on up on the rare book market.) Over 1,200 illustrations. xiii + 153pp. 7¾ x 10¾.

T908 Paperbound $2.00

*THE CRAFTSMAN'S HANDBOOK, Cennino Cennini.* The finest English translation of IL LIBRO DELL' ARTE, the 15th century introduction to art technique that is both a mirror of Quatrocento life and a source of many useful but nearly forgotten facets of the painter's art. 4 illustrations. xxvii + 142pp. D. V. Thompson, translator. 5⅜ x 8.

T54 Paperbound $1.35

*THE BROWN DECADES, Lewis Mumford.* A picture of the "buried renaissance" of the post-Civil War period, and the founding of modern architecture (Sullivan, Richardson, Root, Roebling), landscape development (Marsh, Olmstead, Eliot), and the graphic arts (Homer, Eakins, Ryder). 2nd revised, enlarged edition. Bibliography. 12 illustrations. xiv + 266 pp. 5⅜ x 8.

T200 Paperbound $1.75

*THE HUMAN FIGURE, J. H. Vanderpoel.* Not just a picture book, but a complete course by a famous figure artist. Extensive text, illustrated by 430 pencil and charcoal drawings of both male and female anatomy. 2nd enlarged edition. Foreword. 430 illus. 143pp. 6⅛ x 9¼.

T432 Paperbound $1.45

*PINE FURNITURE OF EARLY NEW ENGLAND, R. H. Kettell.* Over 400 illustrations, over 50 working drawings of early New England chairs, benches, beds, cupboards, mirrors, shelves, tables, other furniture esteemed for simple beauty and character. "Rich store of illustrations . . . emphasizes the individuality and varied design," ANTIQUES. 413 illustrations, 55 working drawings. 475pp. 8 x 10¾.

T145 Clothbound $10.00

# Dover Books on Art

*HAWTHORNE ON PAINTING.* Vivid re-creation, from students' notes, of instructions by Charles Hawthorne at Cape Cod School of Art. Essays, epigrammatic comments on color, form, seeing, techniques, etc. "Excellent," Time. 100pp. 5⅜ x 8.

T653 Paperbound $1.00

*THE HANDBOOK OF PLANT AND FLORAL ORNAMENT, R. G. Hatton.* 1200 line illustrations, from medieval, Renaissance herbals, of flowering or fruiting plants: garden flowers, wild flowers, medicinal plants, poisons, industrial plants, etc. A unique compilation that probably could not be matched in any library in the world. Formerly "The Craftsman's Plant-Book." Also full text on uses, history as ornament, etc. 548pp. 6⅛ x 9¼.

T649 Paperbound $3.00

*DECORATIVE ALPHABETS AND INITIALS, Alexander Nesbitt.* 91 complete alphabets, over 3900 ornamental initials, from Middle Ages, Renaissance printing, baroque, rococo, and modern sources. Individual items copyright free, for use in commercial art, crafts, design, packaging, etc. 123 full-page plates. 3924 initials. 129pp. 7¾ x 10¾.

T544 Paperbound $2.25

*METHODS AND MATERIALS OF THE GREAT SCHOOLS AND MASTERS, Sir Charles Eastlake.* (Formerly titled "Materials for a History of Oil Painting.") Vast, authentic reconstruction of secret techniques of the masters, recreated from ancient manuscripts, contemporary accounts, analysis of paintings, etc. Oils, fresco, tempera, varnishes, encaustics. Both Flemish and Italian schools, also British and French. One of great works for art historians, critics; inexhaustible mine of suggestions, information for practicing artists. Total of 1025pp. 5⅜ x 8.

Two volume set, T718-9 Paperbound $4.50

*BYZANTINE ART AND ARCHAEOLOGY, O. M. Dalton.* Still most thorough work in English on Byzantine art forms throughout ancient and medieval world. Analyzes hundreds of pieces, covers sculpture, painting, mosaic, jewelry, textiles, architecture, etc. Historical development; specific examples; iconology and ideas; symbolism. A treasure-trove of material about one of most important art traditions, will supplement and expand any other book in area. Bibliography of over 2500 items. 457 illustrations. 747pp. 6⅛ x 9¼.

T776 Clothbound $8.50

# Dover Books on Art

*FOOT-HIGH LETTERS: A GUIDE TO LETTERING, M. Price.*
28 15½ x 22½" plates, give classic Roman alphabet, one foot
high per letter, plus 9 other 2" high letter forms for each letter.
16 page syllabus. Ideal for lettering classes, home study. 28 plates
in box.                                                    T239 $6.00

*A HANDBOOK OF WEAVES, G. H. Oelsner.* Most complete
book of weaves, fully explained, differentiated, illustrated. Plain
weaves, irregular, double-stitched, filling satins; derivative,
basket, rib weaves; steep, broken, herringbone, twills, lace, tricot,
many others. Translated, revised by S. S. Dale; supplement on
analysis of weaves. Bible for all handweavers. 1875 illustrations.
410pp. 6⅛ x 9¼.                                 T209 Clothbound $5.00

*JAPANESE HOMES AND THEIR SURROUNDINGS, E. S.
Morse.* Classic describes, analyses, illustrates all aspects of traditional Japanese home, from plan and structure to appoint-
ments, furniture, etc. Published in 1886, before Japanese architecture was contaminated by Western, this is strikingly modern
in beautiful, functional approach to living. Indispensable to every
architect, interior decorator, designer. 307 illustrations. Glossary.
410pp. 5⅝ x 8⅜.                                T746 Paperbound $2.25

*THE DRAWINGS OF HEINRICH KLEY.* Uncut publication of
long-sought-after sketchbooks of satiric, ironic iconoclast. Remarkable fantasy, weird symbolism, brilliant technique make
Kley a shocking experience to layman, endless source of ideas,
techniques for artist. 200 drawings, original size, captions translated. Introduction. 136pp. 6 x 9.            T24 Paperbound $1.65

*COSTUMES OF THE ANCIENTS, Thomas Hope.* Beautiful,
clear, sharp line drawings of Greek and Roman figures in full
costume, by noted artist and antiquary of early 19th century.
Dress, armor, divinities, masks, etc. Invaluable sourcebook for
costumers, designers, first-rate picture file for illustrators, commercial artists. Introductory text by Hope. 300 plates. 6 x 9.
                                               T21 Paperbound $2.00

*VITRUVIUS: TEN BOOKS ON ARCHITECTURE.* The most
influential book in the history of architecture. 1st century A.D.
Roman classic has influenced such men as Bramante, Palladio,
Michelangelo, up to present. Classic principles of design, har-
mony, etc. Fascinating reading. Definitive English translation by
Professor H. Morgan, Harvard. 344pp. 5⅜ x 8.
                                               T645 Paperbound $2.00

# Dover Books on Art

*THE BOOK OF SIGNS, R. Koch.* 493 symbols—crosses, monograms, astrological, biological symbols, runes, etc.—from ancient manuscripts, cathedrals, coins, catacombs, pottery. May be reproduced permission-free. 493 illustrations by Fritz Kredel. 104pp. 6⅛ x 9¼. **T162 Paperbound $1.00**

*A HANDBOOK OF EARLY ADVERTISING ART, C. P. Hornung.* The largest collection of copyright-free early advertising art ever compiled. Vol. I: 2,000 illustrations of animals, old automobiles, buildings, allegorical figures, fire engines, Indians, ships, trains, more than 33 other categories! Vol. II: Over 4,000 typographical specimens; 600 Roman, Gothic, Barnum, Old English faces; 630 ornamental type faces; hundreds of scrolls, initials, flourishes, etc. "A remarkable collection," PRINTERS' INK.

Vol. I: Pictorial Volume. Over 2000 illustrations. 256pp. 9 x 12.
**T122 Clothbound $10.00**

Vol. II: Typographical Volume. Over 4000 specimens. 319pp. 9 x 12.
**T123 Clothbound $10.00**
Two volume set, Clothbound, only **$18.50**

*THE AUTOBIOGRAPHY OF AN IDEA, Louis Sullivan.* The architect whom Frank Lloyd Wright called "the master," records the development of the theories that revolutionized America's skyline. 34 full-page plates of Sullivan's finest work. New introduction by R. M. Line. xiv + 335pp. 5⅜ x 8.
**T281 Paperbound $2.00**

*THE MATERIALS AND TECHNIQUES OF MEDIEVAL PAINTING, D. V. Thompson.* An invaluable study of carriers and grounds, binding media, pigments, metals used in painting, al fresco and al secco techniques, burnishing, etc. used by the medieval masters. Preface by Bernard Berenson. 239pp. 5⅜ x 8.
**T327 Paperbound $1.85**

*HANDBOOK OF ORNAMENT, F. S. Meyer.* One of the largest collections of copyright-free traditional art: over 3300 line cuts of Greek, Roman, Medieval, Renaissance, Baroque, 18th and 19th century art motifs (tracery, geometric elements, flower and animal motifs, etc.) and decorated objects (chairs, thrones, weapons, vases, jewelry, armor, etc.). Full text. 300 plates. 3300 illustrations. 562pp. 5⅜ x 8. **T302 Paperbound $2.50**

# Dover Books on Art

*LANDSCAPE GARDENING IN JAPAN, Josiah Conder.* A detailed picture of Japanese gardening techniques and ideas, the artistic principles incorporated in the Japanese garden, and the religious and ethical concepts at the heart of those principles. Preface. 92 illustrations, plus all 40 full-page plates from the Supplement. Index. xv + 299pp. 8⅜ x 11¼.

T1216 Paperbound $2.75

*DESIGN AND FIGURE CARVING, E. J. Tangerman.* "Anyone who can peel a potato can carve," states the author, and in this unusual book he shows you how, covering every stage in detail from very simple exercises working up to museum-quality pieces. Terrific aid for hobbyists, arts and crafts counselors, teachers, those who wish to make reproductions for the commercial market. Appendix: How to Enlarge a Design. Brief bibliography. Index. 1298 figures. x + 289pp. 5⅜ x 8½.

T1209 Paperbound $1.85

*WILD FOWL DECOYS, Joel Barber.* Antique dealers, collectors, craftsmen, hunters, readers of Americana, etc. will find this the only thorough and reliable guide on the market today to this unique folk art. It contains the history, cultural significance, regional design variations; unusual decoy lore; working plans for constructing decoys; and loads of illustrations. 140 full-page plates, 4 in color. 14 additional plates of drawings and plans by the author. xxvii + 156pp. 7⅞ x 10¾.     T11 Paperbound $2.75

*1800 WOODCUTS BY THOMAS BEWICK AND HIS SCHOOL.* This is the largest collection of first-rate pictorial woodcuts in print—an indispensable part of the working library of every commercial artist, art director, production designer, packaging artist, craftsman, manufacturer, librarian, art collector, and artist. And best of all, when you buy your copy of Bewick, you buy the rights to reproduce individual illustrations—no permission needed, no acknowledgments, no clearance fees! Classified index. Bibliography and sources. xiv + 246pp. 9 x 12.

T766 Clothbound $10.00

*THE SCRIPT LETTER, Tommy Thompson.* Prepared by a noted authority, this is a thorough, straightforward course of instruction with advice on virtually every facet of the art of script lettering. Also a brief history of lettering with examples from early copy books and illustrations from present day advertising and packaging. Copiously illustrated. Bibliography. 128pp. 6½ x 9⅛.

T1311 Paperbound $1.00

# Dover Books on Art

*AFRICAN SCULPTURE, Ladislas Segy.* 163 full-page plates illustrating masks, fertility figures, ceremonial objects, etc., of 50 West and Central African tribes—95% never before illustrated. 34-page introduction to African sculpture. "Mr. Segy is one of its top authorities," NEW YORKER. 164 full-page photographic plates. Introduction. Bibliography. 244pp. 6⅛ x 9¼.

T396 Paperbound $2.00

*CALLIGRAPHY, J. G. Schwandner.* First reprinting in 200 years of this legendary book of beautiful handwriting. Over 300 ornamental initials, 12 complete calligraphic alphabets, over 150 ornate frames and panels, 75 calligraphic pictures of cherubs, stags, lions, etc., thousands of flourishes, scrolls, etc., by the greatest 18th-century masters. All material can be copied or adapted without permission. Historical introduction. 158 full-page plates. 368pp. 9 x 13. T475 Clothbound $10.00

*A DIDEROT PICTORIAL ENCYCLOPEDIA OF TRADES AND INDUSTRY.* Manufacturing and the Technical Arts in Plates Selected from "L'Encyclopédie ou Dictionnaire Raisonné des Sciences, des Arts, et des Métiers," of Denis Diderot, edited with text by C. Gillispie. Over 2000 illustrations on 485 full-page plates. Magnificent 18th-century engravings of men, women, and children working at such trades as milling flour, cheesemaking, charcoal burning, mining, silverplating, shoeing horses, making fine glass, printing, hundreds more, showing details of machinery, different steps in sequence, etc. A remarkable art work, but also the largest collection of working figures in print, copyright-free, for art directors, designers, etc. Two vols. 920pp. 9 x 12. Heavy library cloth. T421 Two volume set $18.50

*SILK SCREEN TECHNIQUES, J. Biegeleisen, M. Cohn.* A practical step-by-step home course in one of the most versatile, least expensive graphic arts processes. How to build an inexpensive silk screen, prepare stencils, print, achieve special textures, use color, etc. Every step explained, diagrammed. 149 illustrations, 201pp. 6⅛ x 9¼. T433 Paperbound $1.55

*STICKS AND STONES, Lewis Mumford.* An examination of forces influencing American architecture: the medieval tradition in early New England, the classical influence in Jefferson's time, the Brown Decades, the imperial facade, the machine age, etc. "A truly remarkable book," SAT. REV. OF LITERATURE. 2nd revised edition. 21 illus. xvii + 240pp. 5⅜ x 8.

T202 Paperbound $1.65

# Dover Books on Art

*PRINCIPLES OF ART HISTORY, H. Wölfflin.* This remarkably instructive work demonstrates the tremendous change in artistic conception from the 14th to the 18th centuries, by analyzing 164 works by Botticelli, Dürer, Hobbema, Holbein, Hals, Titian, Rembrandt, Vermeer, etc., and pointing out exactly what is meant by "baroque," "classic," "primitive," "picturesque," and other basic terms of art history and criticism. "A remarkable lesson in the art of seeing," SAT. REV. OF LITERATURE. Translated from the 7th German edition. 150 illus. 254pp. 6⅛ x 9¼.                                     T276 Paperbound $2.00

*FOUNDATIONS OF MODERN ART, A. Ozenfant.* Stimulating discussion of human creativity from paleolithic cave painting to modern painting, architecture, decorative arts. Fully illustrated with works of Gris, Lipchitz, Léger, Picasso, primitive, modern artifacts, architecture, industrial art, much more. 226 illustrations. 368pp. 6⅛ x 9¼.            T215 Paperbound $2.00

*METALWORK AND ENAMELLING, H. Maryon.* Probably the best book ever written on the subject. Tells everything necessary for the home manufacture of jewelry, rings, ear pendants, bowls, etc. Covers materials, tools, soldering, filigree, setting stones, raising patterns, repoussé work, damascening, niello, cloisonné, polishing, assaying, casting, and dozens of other techniques. The best substitute for apprenticeship to a master metalworker. 363 photos and figures. 374pp. 5½ x 8½.
T183 Clothbound $8.50

*SHAKER FURNITURE, E. D. and F. Andrews.* The most illuminating study of Shaker furniture ever written. Covers chronology, craftsmanship, houses, shops, etc. Includes over 200 photographs of chairs, tables, clocks, beds, benches, etc. "Mr. & Mrs. Andrews know all there is to know about Shaker furniture," Mark Van Doren, NATION. 48 full-page plates. 192pp. 7⅞ x 10¾.                                T679 Paperbound $2.00

*ANIMAL DRAWING: ANATOMY AND ACTION FOR ARTISTS, C. R. Knight.* 158 studies, with full accompanying text, of such animals as the gorilla, bear, bison, dromedary, camel, vulture, pelican, iguana, shark, etc., by one of the greatest modern masters of animal drawing. Innumerable tips on how to get life expression into your work. "An excellent reference work," SAN FRANCISCO CHRONICLE. 158 illustrations. 156pp. 10½ x 8½.                                     T426 Paperbound $2.00

# Dover Books on Art

*THE HISTORY AND TECHNIQUE OF LETTERING, A. Nesbitt.* A thorough history of lettering from the ancient Egyptians to the present, and a 65-page course in lettering for artists. Every major development in lettering history is illustrated by a complete aphabet. Fully analyzes such masters as Caslon, Koch, Garamont, Jenson, and many more. 89 alphabets, 165 other specimens. 317pp. 7½ x 10½.                   T427 Paperbound $2.00

*LETTERING AND ALPHABETS, J. A. Cavanagh.* An unabridged reissue of "Lettering," containing the full discussion, analysis, illustration of 89 basic hand lettering styles based on Caslon, Bodoni, Gothic, many other types. Hundreds of technical hints on construction, strokes, pens, brushes, etc. 89 alphabets, 72 lettered specimens, which may be reproduced permission-free. 121pp. 9¾ x 8.                         T53 Paperbound $1.35

*THE HUMAN FIGURE IN MOTION, Eadweard Muybridge.* The largest collection in print of Muybridge's famous high-speed action photos. 4789 photographs in more than 500 action-strip-sequences (at shutter speeds up to 1/6000th of a second) illustrate men, women, children—mostly undraped—performing such actions as walking, running, getting up, lying down,.carrying objects, throwing, etc. "An unparalleled dictionary of action for all artists," AMERICAN ARTIST. 390 full-page plates, with 4789 photographs. Heavy glossy stock, reinforced binding with headbands. 7⅞ x 10¾.                T204 Clothbound $10.00

*ANIMALS IN MOTION, Eadweard Muybridge.* The largest collection of animal action photos in print. 34 different animals (horses, mules, oxen, goats, camels, pigs, cats, lions, gnus, deer, monkeys, eagles—and 22 others) in 132 characteristic actions. All 3919 photographs are taken in series at speeds up to 1/1600th of a second, offering artists, biologists, cartoonists a remarkable opportunity to see exactly how an ostrich's head bobs when running, how a lion puts his foot down, how an elephant's knee bends, how a bird flaps his wings, thousands of other hard-to-catch details. "A really marvellous series of plates," NATURE. 380 full-page plates. Heavy glossy stock, reinforced binding with headbands. 7⅞ x 10¾.                 T203 Clothbound $10.00

*BASIC BOOKBINDING, A. W. Lewis.* Enables both beginners and experts to rebind old books or bind paperbacks in hard covers. Treats materials, tools; gives step-by-step instruction in how to collate a book, sew it, back it, make boards, etc. 261 illus. Appendices. 155pp. 5⅜ x 8.               T169 Paperbound $1.45

*200 DECORATIVE TITLE-PAGES, edited by A. Nesbitt.* Fascinating and informative from a historical point of view, this beautiful collection of decorated titles will be a great inspiration to students of design, commercial artists, advertising designers, etc. A complete survey of the genre from the first known decorated title to work in the first decades of this century. Bibliography and sources of the plates. 222pp. 8⅜ x 11¼.

T1264 Paperbound $2.75

*ON THE LAWS OF JAPANESE PAINTING, H. P. Bowie.* This classic work on the philosophy and technique of Japanese art is based on the author's first-hand experiences studying art in Japan. Every aspect of Japanese painting is described: the use of the brush and other materials; laws governing conception and execution; subjects for Japanese paintings, etc. The best possible substitute for a series of lessons from a great Oriental master. Index. xv + 117pp. + 66 plates. 6⅛ x 9¼.

T30 Paperbound $2.00

*PAINTING IN THE FAR EAST, L. Binyon.* A study of over 1500 years of Oriental art by one of the world's outstanding authorities. The author chooses the most important masters in each period—Wu Tao-tzu, Toba Sojo, Kanaoka, Li Lung-mien, Masanobu, Okio, etc.—and examines the works, schools, and influence of each within their cultural context. 42 photographs. Sources of original works and selected bibliography. Notes including list of principal painters by periods. xx + 297pp. 6⅛ x 9¼.

T520 Paperbound $2.25

*THE ALPHABET AND ELEMENTS OF LETTERING, F. W. Goudy.* A beautifully illustrated volume on the aesthetics of letters and type faces and their history and development. Each plate consists of 15 forms of a single letter with the last plate devoted to the ampersand and the numerals. "A sound guide for all persons engaged in printing or drawing," Saturday Review. 27 full-page plates. 48 additional figures. xii + 131pp. 7⅞ x 10¾.

T792 Paperbound $2.00

*PAINTING IN ISLAM, Sir Thomas W. Arnold.* This scholarly study puts Islamic painting in its social and religious context and examines its relation to Islamic civilization in general. 65 full-page plates illustrate the text and give outstanding examples of Islamic art. 4 appendices. Index of mss. referred to. General Index. xxiv + 159pp. 6⅝ x 9¼.　　T1310 Paperbound $2.50

# Dover Books on Art

*THE FOUR BOOKS OF ARCHITECTURE, Andrea Palladio.*
A compendium of the art of Andrea Palladio, one of the most celebrated architects of the Renaissance, including 250 magnificently-engraved plates showing edifices either of Palladio's design or reconstructed (in these drawings) by him from classical ruins and contemporary accounts. 257 plates. xxiv + 119pp. 9½ x 12¾.                     T1308 Clothbound $10.00

*150 MASTERPIECES OF DRAWING, A. Toney.* Selected by a gifted artist and teacher, these are some of the finest drawings produced by Western artists from the early 15th to the end of the 18th centuries. Excellent reproductions of drawings by Rembrandt, Bruegel, Raphael, Watteau, and other familiar masters, as well as works by lesser known but brilliant artists. 150 plates. xviii + 150pp. 5⅜ x 11¼.           T1032 Paperbound $2.00

*MORE DRAWINGS BY HEINRICH KLEY.* Another collection of the graphic, vivid sketches of Heinrich Kley, one of the most diabolically talented cartoonists of our century. The sketches take in every aspect of human life: nothing is too sacred for him to ridicule, no one too eminent for him to satirize. 158 drawings you will not easily forget. iv + 104pp. 7⅜ x 10¾.
                                      T41 Paperbound $1.85

*THE TRIUMPH OF MAXIMILIAN I, 137 Woodcuts by Hans Burgkmair and Others.* This is one of the world's great art monuments, a series of magnificent woodcuts executed by the most important artists in the German realms as part of an elaborate plan by Maximilian I, ruler of the Holy Roman Empire, to commemorate his own name, dynasty, and achievements. 137 plates. New translation of descriptive text, notes, and bibliography prepared by Stanley Appelbaum. Special section of 10pp. containing a reduced version of the entire Triumph. x + 169pp. 11⅛ x 9¼.              T1207 Paperbound $3.00

*LOST EXAMPLES OF COLONIAL ARCHITECTURE, J. M. Howells.* This book offers a unique guided tour through America's architectural past, all of which is either no longer in existence or so changed that its original beauty has been destroyed. More than 275 clear photos of old churches, dwelling houses, public buildings, business structures, etc. 245 plates, containing 281 photos and 9 drawings, floorplans, etc. New Index. xvii + 248pp. 7⅞ x 10¾.                    T1143 Paperbound $2.75

# Dover Books on Art

*HANDBOOK OF DESIGNS AND DEVICES, C. P. Hornung.* A remarkable working collection of 1836 basic designs and variations, all copyright-free. Variations of circle, line, cross, diamond, swastika, star, scroll, shield, many more. Notes on symbolism. "A necessity to every designer who would be original without having to labor heavily," ARTIST AND ADVERTISER. 204 plates. 240pp. 5⅜ x 8. **T125 Paperbound $1.90**

*THE UNIVERSAL PENMAN, George Bickham.* Exact reproduction of beautiful 18th-century book of handwriting. 22 complete alphabets in finest English roundhand, other scripts, over 2000 elaborate flourishes, 122 calligraphic illustrations, etc. Material is copyright-free. "An essential part of any art library, and a book of permanent value," AMERICAN ARTIST. 212 plates. 224pp. 9 x 13¾. **T20 Clothbound $10.00**

*AN ATLAS OF ANATOMY FOR ARTISTS, F. Schider.* This standard work contains 189 full-page plates, more than 647 illustrations of all aspects of the human skeleton, musculature, cutaway portions of the body, each part of the anatomy, hand forms, eyelids, breasts, location of muscles under the flesh, etc. 59 plates illustrate how Michelangelo, da Vinci, Goya, 15 others, drew human anatomy. New 3rd edition enlarged by 52 new illustrations by Cloquet, Barcsay. "The standard reference tool," AMERICAN LIBRARY ASSOCIATION. "Excellent," AMERICAN ARTIST. 189 plates, 647 illustrations. xxvi + 192pp. 7⅞ x 10⅝. **T241 Clothbound $6.00**

*AN ATLAS OF ANIMAL ANATOMY FOR ARTISTS, W. Ellenberger, H. Baum, H. Dittrich.* The largest, richest animal anatomy for artists in English. Form, musculature, tendons, bone structure, expression, detailed cross sections of head, other features, of the horse, lion, dog, cat, deer, seal, kangaroo, cow, bull, goat, monkey, hare, many other animals. "Highly recommended," DESIGN. Second, revised, enlarged edition with new plates from Cuvier, Stubbs, etc. 288 illustrations. 153pp. 11⅜ x 9. **T82 Clothbound $6.00**

*VASARI ON TECHNIQUE, G. Vasari.* Pupil of Michelangelo, outstanding biographer of Renaissance artists reveals technical methods of his day. Marble, bronze, fresco painting, mosaics, engraving, stained glass, rustic ware, etc. Only English translation, extensively annotated by G. Baldwin Brown. 18 plates. 342pp. 5⅜ x 8. **T717 Paperbound $2.00**

# Dover Books on Art

*A HANDBOOK OF ANATOMY FOR ART STUDENTS, Arthur Thomson.* This long-popular text teaches any student, regardless of level of technical competence, all the subtleties of human anatomy. Clear photographs, numerous line sketches and diagrams of bones, joints, etc. Use it as a text for home study, as a supplement to life class work, or as a lifelong sourcebook and reference volume. Author's prefaces. 67 plates, containing 40 line drawings, 86 photographs—mostly full page. 211 figures. Appendix. Index. xx + 459pp. 5⅜ x 8⅜. T1163 Paperbound $3.00

*WHITTLING AND WOODCARVING, E. J. Tangerman.* With this book, a beginner who is moderately handy can whittle or carve scores of useful objects, toys for children, gifts, or simply pass hours creatively and enjoyably. "Easy as well as instructive reading," N. Y. Herald Tribune Books. 464 illustrations, with appendix and index. x + 293pp. 5½ x 8⅛.
T965 Paperbound $1.75

*ONE HUNDRED AND ONE PATCHWORK PATTERNS, Ruby Short McKim.* Whether you have made a hundred quilts or none at all, you will find this the single most useful book on quiltmaking. There are 101 full patterns (all exact size) with full instructions for cutting and sewing. In addition there is some really choice folklore about the origin of the ingenious pattern names: "Monkey Wrench," "Road to California," "Drunkard's Path," "Crossed Canoes," to name a few. Over 500 illustrations. 124 pp. 7⅞ x 10¾. T773 Paperbound $1.85

*ART AND GEOMETRY, W. M. Ivins, Jr.* Challenges the idea that the foundations of modern thought were laid in ancient Greece. Pitting Greek tactile-muscular intuitions of space against modern visual intuitions, the author, for 30 years curator of prints, Metropolitan Museum of Art, analyzes the differences between ancient and Renaissance painting and sculpture and tells of the first fruitful investigations of perspective. x + 113pp. 5⅜ x 8⅜. T941 Paperbound $1.00

*TEACH YOURSELF TO STUDY SCULPTURE, Wm. Gaunt.* Useful details on the sculptor's art and craft, tools, carving and modeling; its relation to other arts; ways to look at sculpture; sculpture of the East and West; etc. "Useful both to the student and layman and a good refresher for the professional sculptor," Prof. J. Skeaping, Royal College of Art. 32 plates, 24 figures. Index. xii + 155pp. 7 x 4¼. Clothbound $2.00

# Dover Books on Art

*THE STYLES OF ORNAMENT, A. Speltz.* The largest collection of line ornament in print, with 3750 numbered illustrations arranged chronologically from Egypt, Assyria, Greeks, Romans, Etruscans, through Medieval, Renaissance, 18th century, and Victorian. No permissions, no fees needed to use or reproduce illustrations. 400 plates with 3750 illustrations. Bibliography. Index. 640pp. 6 x 9.                      T577 Paperbound $2.50

*THE ART OF ETCHING, E. S. Lumsden.* Every step of the etching process from essential materials to completed proof is carefully and clearly explained, with 24 annotated plates exemplifying every technique and approach discussed. The book also features a rich survey of the art, with 105 annotated plates by masters. Invaluable for beginner to advanced etcher. 374pp. 5⅜ x 8.                           T49 Paperbound $2.50

*EPOCHS OF CHINESE AND JAPANESE ART, E. Fenollosa.* Classic study of pre-20th century Oriental art, revealing, as does no other book, the important interrelationships between the art of China and Japan and their history and sociology. Illustrations include ancient bronzes, Buddhist paintings by Kobo Daishi, scroll paintings by Toba Sojo, prints by Nobusane, screens by Korin, woodcuts by Hokusai, Koryusai, Utamaro, Hiroshige and scores of other pieces by Chinese and Japanese masters. Biographical preface. Notes. Index. 242 illustrations. Total of lii + 439pp. plus 174 plates. 5⅝ x 8¼.
Two-volume set, T364-5 Paperbound $5.00

*OF THE JUST SHAPING OF LETTERS, Albrecht Dürer.* This remarkable volume reveals Albrecht Dürer's rules for the geometric construction of Roman capitals and the formation of Gothic lower case and capital letters, complete with construction diagrams and directions. Of considerable practical interest to the contemporary illustrator, artist, and designer. Translated from the Latin text of the edition of 1535 by R. T. Nichol. Numerous letterform designs, construction diagrams, illustrations. iv + 43pp. 7⅞ x 10¾.                      T1306 Paperbound $1.25

*DESIGN MOTIFS OF ANCIENT MEXICO, J. Enciso.* Nearly 90% of these 766 superb designs frqm Aztec, Olmec, Totonac, Maya, and Toltec origins are unobtainable elsewhere. Contains plumed serpents, wind gods, animals, demons, dancers, monsters, etc. Excellent applied design source. Originally $17.50. 766 illustrations, thousands of motifs. 192pp. 6⅛ x 9¼.
T84 Paperbound $1.85

# Dover Books on Art

*MASTERPIECES OF FURNITURE, Verna Cook Salomonsky.*
Photographs and measured drawings of some of the finest examples of Colonial American, 17th century English, Windsor, Sheraton, Hepplewhite, Chippendale, Louis XIV, Queen Anne, and various other furniture styles. The textual matter includes information on traditions, characteristics, background, etc. of various pieces. 101 plates. Bibliography. 224pp. 7⅞ x 10¾.
T1381 Paperbound $2.00

*PRIMITIVE ART, Franz Boas.* In this exhaustive volume, a great American anthropologist analyzes all the fundamental traits of primitive art, covering the formal element in art, representative art, symbolism, style, literature, music, and the dance. Illustrations of Indian embroidery, paleolithic paintings, woven blankets, wing and tail designs, totem poles, cutlery, earthenware, baskets and many other primitive objects and motifs. Over 900 illustrations. 376pp. 5⅜ x 8.　　　　T25 Paperbound $2.00

*AN INTRODUCTION TO A HISTORY OF WOODCUT, A. M. Hind.* Nearly all of this authoritative 2-volume set is devoted to the 15th century—the period during which the woodcut came of age as an important art form. It is the most complete compendium of information on this period, the artists who contributed to it, and their technical and artistic accomplishments. Profusely illustrated with cuts by 15th century masters, and later works for comparative purposes. 484 illustrations. 5 indexes. Total of xi + 838pp. 5⅜ x 8½. Two-volume set, T952-3 Paperbound $5.00

*ART STUDENTS' ANATOMY, E. J. Farris.* Teaching anatomy by using chiefly living objects for illustration, this study has enjoyed long popularity and success in art courses and home-study programs. All the basic elements of the human anatomy are illustrated in minute detail, diagrammed and pictured as they pass through common movements and actions. 158 drawings, photographs, and roentgenograms. Glossary of anatomical terms. x + 159pp. 5⅝ x 8⅜.　　　　T744 Paperbound $1.50

*COLONIAL LIGHTING, A. H. Hayward.* The only book to cover the fascinating story of lamps and other lighting devices in America. Beginning with rush light holders used by the early settlers, it ranges through the elaborate chandeliers of the Federal period, illustrating 647 lamps. Of great value to antique collectors, designers, and historians of arts and crafts. Revised and enlarged by James R. Marsh. xxxi + 198pp. 5⅝ x 8¼.
T975 Paperbound $2.00

# Dover Books on Art

*GREEK REVIVAL ARCHITECTURE IN AMERICA, T. Hamlin.* A comprehensive study of the American Classical Revival, its regional variations, reasons for its success and eventual decline. Profusely illustrated with photos, sketches, floor plans and sections, displaying the work of almost every important architect of the time. 2 appendices. 39 figures, 94 plates containing 221 photos, 62 architectural designs, drawings, etc. 324-item classified bibliography. Index. xi + 439pp. 5⅜ x 8½.

T1148 Paperbound $3.00

*CREATIVE LITHOGRAPHY AND HOW TO DO IT, Grant Arnold.* Written by a man who practiced and taught lithography for many years, this highly useful volume explains all the steps of the lithographic process from tracing the drawings on the stone to printing the lithograph, with helpful hints for solving special problems. Index. 16 reproductions of lithographs. 11 drawings. xv + 214pp. of text. 5⅜ x 8½.

T1208 Paperbound $1.65

*TEACH YOURSELF ANTIQUE COLLECTING, E. Bradford.* An excellent, brief guide to collecting British furniture, silver, pictures and prints, pewter, pottery and porcelain, Victoriana, enamels, clocks or other antiques. Much background information difficult to find elsewhere. 15pp. of illus. 215pp. 7 x 4¼.

Clothbound $2.00

*THE STANDARD BOOK OF QUILT MAKING AND COLLECTING, M. Ickis.* Even if you are a beginner, you will soon find yourself quilting like an expert, by following these clearly drawn patterns, photographs, and step-by-step instructions. Learn how to plan the quilt, to select the pattern to harmonize with the design and color of the room, to choose materials. Over 40 full-size patterns. Index. 483 illustrations. One color plate. xi + 276pp. 6¾ x 9½.       T582 Paperbound $2.00

*THE ENJOYMENT AND USE OF COLOR, W. Sargent.* Requiring no special technical know-how, this book tells you all about color and how it is created, perceived, and imitated in art. Covers many little-known facts about color values, intensities, effects of high and low illumination, complementary colors, and color harmonies. Simple do-it-yourself experiments and observations. 35 illustrations, including 6 full-page color plates. New color frontispiece. Index. x + 274 pp. 5⅜ x 8.

T944 Paperbound $2.00

# Dover Books on Art

*THE COMPLETE BOOK OF SILK SCREEN PRINTING PRO-DUCTION, J. I. Biegeleisen.* Here is a clear and complete picture of every aspect of silk screen technique and press operation—from individually operated manual presses to modern automatic ones. Unsurpassed as a guidebook for setting up shop, making shop operation more efficient, finding out about latest methods and equipment; or as a textbook for use in teaching, studying, or learning all aspects of the profession. 124 figures. Index. Bibliography. List of Supply Sources. xi + 253pp. 5⅜ x 8½.

T1100 Paperbound $2.00

*A HISTORY OF COSTUME, Carl Köhler.* The most reliable and authentic account of the development of dress from ancient times through the 19th century. Based on actual pieces of clothing that have survived, using paintings, statues and other reproductions only where originals no longer exist. Hundreds of illustrations, including detailed patterns for many articles. Highly useful for theatre and movie directors, fashion designers, illustrators, teachers. Edited and augmented by Emma von Sichart. Translated by Alexander K. Dallas. 594 illustrations. 464pp. 5⅛ x 7⅛.

T1030 Paperbound $2.75

*CHINESE HOUSEHOLD FURNITURE, G. N. Kates.* A summary of virtually everything that is known about authentic Chinese furniture before it was contaminated by the influence of the West. The text covers history of styles, materials used, principles of design and craftsmanship, and furniture arrangement—all fully illustrated. xiii + 190pp. 5⅝ x 8½.

T958 Paperbound $1.50

*THE COMPLETE WOODCUTS OF ALBRECHT DURER,* edited by Dr. Willi Kurth. Albrecht Dürer was a master in various media, but it was in woodcut design that his creative genius reached its highest expression. Here are all of his extant woodcuts, a collection of over 300 great works, many of which are not available elsewhere. An indispensable work for the art historian and critic and all art lovers. 346 plates. Index. 285pp. 8½ x 12¼.

T1097 Paperbound $2.50

---